A Modern Approach to English Grammar

A Modern Approach to English Grammar

An Introduction to Systemic Grammar

James Muir

B. T. Batsford Ltd
London

First published 1972
© James Muir 1972

Printed and bound in Great Britain by
Richard Clay (The Chaucer Press) Ltd,
Bungay, Suffolk
for the publishers
B. T. BATSFORD LTD
4 Fitzhardinge Street, London W1H OAH

ISBN O 7134 2008 1

To the memory of O.K.S.

Contents

Preface

This book is intended to present a description of English grammar which is based on a particular theory or 'model' of linguistics. This model has been known as 'Scale and Category' linguistics, or, more recently (and more appropriately), as 'Systemic' linguistics. Such theoretical foundation is discussed in this book only where necessary, and no discussion of the advantages and disadvantages of this particular model is offered. For those interested in such questions, a highly technical account of the theory will be found in the article 'Categories of the Theory of Grammar' by M. A. K. Halliday, in *Word* (Vol. 17, No. 3, 1961); a fuller and more up-to-date account will be found in *Systemic Linguistics* by H. M. Berry, to be published by B. T. Batsford Ltd. in 1973, which may, in fact, be considered as a theoretical counterpart to this book and which (like this book) is intended for undergraduates, training college students and interested teachers.

This book makes no claim to originality in anything other than in a few places. It provides a reasonably comprehensive description of 'Surface Grammar' (Part 2) and a somewhat less detailed description of 'Deep Grammar' (Part 3). The General Survey (Part 1) is a summation of the other two parts and provides a general (an 'overall') picture of the grammar, which can be enlarged and deepened throughout Parts 2 and 3. Essentially, this book is intended to provide a grammar which is neither an elementary textbook nor an advanced linguistic dissertation. There is a space between these extremes which needs to be filled, both for those who will teach from elementary textbooks and for those who will proceed to more advanced and diverse linguistic study.

Since little is original, I obviously owe much to teachers and colleagues over a number of years. It is perhaps appropriate to mention here particularly the teaching and later the writings of M. A. K. Halliday and J. M. Sinclair, on which much of this book is based. More specific acknowledgement is made elsewhere. I also owe particular thanks, of a somewhat different nature, to Mr. A. R. Thompson, editor of the *Scottish Secondary Schoolteachers' Magazine*, and Mr. J. McGrath of the Language Sub-committee of the Glasgow Education Authority Committee for English, for reading through an early draft and offering helpful comment and advice.

JM

1
General Survey

It is important to be aware that language is always linearly manifested; that is, serial in presentation. In speaking or writing, items follow each other in temporal or spatial succession. But the extra-linguistic phenomena to which language refers may not be sequential; the most commonly observed events are complex, although their various aspects—the interaction of perhaps a number of components which constitutes the whole event—may be perceived simultaneously.

Professor Quirk[1] gives the simple example of a boy patting a dog, and comments:

> We could not readily assign an order to the boy, the patting, the dog, the boy's stoop, the dog's tail. On the other hand, as soon as you try to report what you have seen, you find that you not only can, but *must*, assign an order to it and *must* break up your impression into pieces of your own choosing and present them, not simultaneously, but one by one.

Music and mathematics show us the advantages of simultaneous over serial expression. Professor Quirk invites us to compare $\sqrt[3]{\dfrac{125}{3}}$ with a linguistic form of this expression: 'the cube root of a hundred and twenty five divided by three'. As soon as we do this, however, we become aware that there is, in fact, an order in the serial expression of language. We must, in using the linguistic form of the expression, know how to punctuate it (in writing) or how to modify our voice

(in speaking) in order to ensure that it will be interpreted as $\sqrt[3]{\dfrac{125}{3}}$
and not $\sqrt[3]{125} \div 3$ or even $\sqrt[3]{100} + \dfrac{25}{3}$.

In other words, language—despite its necessarily linear presentation—is patterned activity; it has structure. We must, in the above example, know the linguistic grammar in order to interpret the linguistic expression correctly, just as we must know the mathematical grammar in order to interpret the mathematical expression correctly. A linguistic expression is not just the additive value of words (or of any other unit), but the complex patternings formed by the operation of units within each other. Let us consider two linguistic expressions and their possible patterning:

(i) *twenty two month old babies*
  (*a*) twenty (two month old) babies
  i.e. twenty babies who are two months old
  (*b*) twenty two (month old) babies
  i.e. twenty two babies who are one month old
  (*c*) (twenty two month old) babies
  i.e. babies who are twenty two months old

(ii) *new car salesman*
  (*a*) new (car salesman)
  i.e. a car salesman who is new
  (*b*) new car (salesman)
  i.e. a salesman who sells new cars

It is obvious that these expressions cannot be simply represented as (i) twenty two year old babies; (ii) new car salesman. The completion of Professor Quirk's analogy aptly illustrates this:

A linguistic expression is less like
$$4 + 8 + 7 + 9 + 8 + 6 + 5 + 9 + 4$$
than like
$$[(4 + 2)3] + [3(5 + 7) + 6].$$

Native English speakers will agree that an expression such as
  dog bites man
has three parts or elements. We do not say this because the expression contains three words, but because we recognise a pattern. The same pattern is evident in the expression

(the great big heavy dog) *(bites)* *(the little thin man)*.
We do not say that this expression has ten elements of structure because it has ten words, but rather that it also has three elements.

Language, to repeat, is patterned activity. This means that certain regularities are exhibited over certain stretches of language activity. The grammatical category set up to account for these 'stretches of language' is the unit. A unit may be defined as any stretch of language which exhibits a recognised pattern. The units of a language are of varying extent, and may occur sequentially or be included within each other. The patterns which these units carry take the form of like events, and the category which accounts for likeness of events is the structure. Each unit operates at an element of structure in the unit next above, and the particular configuration of units operating as elements of structure in a given example of a higher unit form the structure of that unit. Thus the expression

1   2   3

(the great big heavy dog) *(bites)* *(the little thin man)*

is a single unit, the structure of which is formed by the elements of structure realised by the three smaller units.

There are, however, restrictions on which units can operate at which elements of structure in the next highest unit; it is not the case that any unit can occur at any place in structure. In English, not all members of the unit 'phrase' can operate at 'predicator' in clause structure, and those which can do so cannot operate elsewhere, say at 'subject'. According to its potentiality of operation in the structure of the unit next above, each unit is assigned a class name.

The two preceding paragraphs have been rather abstract, and perhaps somewhat confusing. Their intent should become clearer in the following pages. The important point to be made at this juncture is that these three categories of unit, class and structure (there is one more to be mentioned a little later) are theoretical categories generally applicable to language and languages. In concerning ourselves henceforth with English, we shall be seeking to discover, define and illustrate the descriptive instances of these categories.

It may be advantageous to break into the description of English by discussing the word *word*, which is a well-known and well-used term for a particular grammatical unit. Traditionally it has been regarded as a basic or central unit; whether or not it should be so regarded (and there are weighty arguments on both sides) it is demonstrably not the lowest unit. Native speakers of English will agree that if we examine the word *unfriendliness* we shall find it is composed of four elements: *un* + *friend* + *li* + *ness*. These elements of structure of the word are realised by members of the unit below the word, and this unit is called the morpheme. A rough working definition of the morpheme is that it is the smallest meaningful unit in language; somewhat more accurately, that it is the smallest unit pertinent to grammatical description. The morpheme is not, however, defined by reference to its meaning; it is identified and defined by the same formal criteria as are applied to other units. If we arrange the units of English on a scale of rank, then the morpheme will be the lowest unit.

A cursory consideration will reveal that there are two main classes or types of morpheme: those which operate (or may operate) without being in association with other morphemes; and those which only occur in association with other morphemes. The former are called free morphemes and the latter are called bound morphemes. Thus:

the word *book* consists of one free morpheme
the word *books* consists of two morphemes; the free morpheme *book* and the bound morpheme *s*
the word *bookish* consists of two morphemes; the free morpheme *book* and the bound morpheme *ish*
the word *bookcase* consists of two morphemes; both are free morphemes and they form a dithematic compound word.

Bound morphemes may be inflexional, as *s* in *books*, or derivational, as *ish* in *bookish*.

Morphemes make up words; words are made up by morphemes. That is, morphemes operate as elements of structure in the next highest unit on the rankscale, which is the word. The structure of any given word will be the configuration of elements of structure realised by morphemes. Each word contains one obligatory element of structure, which is called the base element. Further elements of structure of the word are optional and are dependent on the base; these are called affixes, and further designated prefix, if preceding the base, or postfix, if following the base. We can thus analyse *unfriendliness* as:

Unit: word
Elements of structure: prefix (*un*), base (*friend*), postfix (*li-ness*)
Structure: pbf

At the elements *p* (prefix) and *f* (postfix) operate bound morphemes; at the element *b* (base) operates a free morpheme.

This consideration of morphemes has entailed looking downward from the word and examining how it is made up of smaller constituents. We must now look upward and examine how the word operates in the structure of the next highest unit on the rank-scale.

It has already been observed that the value of a linguistic expression is not just the additive value of the words, but that words enter into groupings:

(*the big dog*) (*bites*) (*the little man*) (*deeply/in the arm*)

The words form into, operate as elements of structure in, these groups. It is convenient to call this next highest unit the group, but the term phrase is also used widely in this meaning; we shall use both terms interchangeably. There are three classes of group in English: nominal group, verbal group and adverbial group; e.g.

nominal group: *the great big dog*; *the little man*; *the boy*; *table*
verbal group: *bites*; *will bite*; *will be biting*; *has bitten*; *bit*
adverbial group: *deeply*; *quickly*; *fast*; *in the field*; *in the arm*.

The nominal group has one obligatory element of structure. This is called the headword or head, as *boy* in the groups *boy*, *the boy*, *the big boy*, *the big boy with red hair*. It is evident from these examples that an element of structure may precede the head element: this is called the modifier; and an element of structure may follow the head element: this is called the qualifier. Thus:

boy is a nominal group with one element of structure, an *h* element, giving the simple structure: *h*

the big boy is a nominal group with two elements of structure, an *m* element (*the big*) and an *h* element (*boy*) giving the structure: *mh*

the big boy with red hair is a nominal group with three elements of structure, an *m* element (*the big*), an *h* element (*boy*) and a *q* element (*with red hair*) giving the structure *mhq*.

At *h* in the nominal group operates the word-class substantive; at *m* in the nominal group various word-classes operate, which may for the present be designated pre-noun; it is not common for single words to operate at *q* in the nominal group.

The verbal group also has one obligatory element of structure; this is called the lexical element, and in the verbal group this is always the final element. The lexical element may be preceded by an element which is called the auxiliar element, and/or by an element which is called the negative element. Thus:

> *comes* is a verbal group with only an *l* element of structure, giving the structure: *l*
> *will come* is a verbal group with two elements of structure, an *a* element (*will*), and an *l* element (*come*), giving the structure: *al*
> *will not come* is a verbal group with three elements of structure, an *a* element (*will*), an *n* element (*not*) and an *l* element (*come*), giving the structure: *anl*.

At *l* in the verbal group operates the word-class lexical verb; at *a* in the verbal group operates the word-class auxiliary verb; at *n* in the verbal group operates the word-class negator.

There are two distinct types of adverbial group in English. In the first type there is again an obligatory element, called the apex. There is an element which may precede this, which is called the temperer, and there is an element which may follow the apex, and this is called the limiter. Thus:

> *sweetly* is an adverbial group with one element of structure, an *a* element, giving the structure: *a*
> *very sweetly* is an adverbial group with two elements of structure, a *t* element (*very*) and an *a* (*sweetly*), giving the structure: *ta*
> *very sweetly indeed* is an adverbial group with three elements of structure, a *t* element (*very*), an *a* element (*sweetly*) and an *l* element (*indeed*), giving the structure: *tal*.

At *t* in the adverbial group operates the word-class sub-modifier; at *a* in the adverbial group operates the word-class adverb; single word items are not characteristic of *l* in the adverbial group.

The second type of adverbial group has two elements of structure, both of which must be present. These are called prepend element and completive element. Thus:

> *on the hill* is an adverbial group with two elements of structure, a *p* element (*on*) and a *c* element (*the hill*), giving the structure: *pc*.

At the element *p* operates the word-class preposition; at *c* operates a complete nominal group.

Groups operate as elements of structure in the next highest unit, which is called the clause. Thus the expression, *the big dog bit the little man on the leg* is one clause with four constituent groups:

1   2   3   4

(the big dog) (bit) (the little man) (on the leg).

To these four elements of structure of the clause we give the traditional names subject, predicator, complement, adjunct. Thus, the clause

the big dog bit the little man on the leg

has four elements of structure, an s element (*the big dog*), a p element (*bit*), a c element (*the little man*) and an A element (*on the leg*), giving a structure: SPCA.

It is important to note that, unlike the elements of structure of the units word and group, the sequence of elements is not fixed in clause structure. Any combination of the four elements may occur; there are clauses with the structures: SPAC, ASPC, PCA, etc. Nominal groups operate at s and c in clause structure; verbal groups operate at p in clause structure; adverbial groups operate at A in clause structure.

There is in English one unit higher than the clause, and this is called the sentence ($\leqq$). The clause operates as an element of structure in the sentence. Thus the sentences

(i) *the big dog bit the little man and he kicked it*

(ii) *the big dog bit the little man because he kicked it*

are each composed of two clauses. The clauses which make up the structure of a sentence may be either independent as in (i) or dependent as *because he kicked it* in (ii).

It is evident from this brief survey that the description of English requires five units, which, arranged on a rankscale of descending magnitude, are:

Sentence
Clause
Group/Phrase
Word
Morpheme.

The relationship which holds between the units on the rankscale is crucial to the grammar here presented: moving from highest to lowest, each unit consists of one or more than one of the next lowest unit. Thus, a sentence consists of one or more than one clause, a

B

clause consists of one or more than one group, a group consists of one or more than one word, a word consists of one or more than one morpheme. Since the structure of each unit is formed by the operation of the next lowest unit, it follows that the lowest unit on the rank-scale, the morpheme, has no (elements of) structure; if it had it would not be the lowest unit.

There are two further points to be made about the rankscale. First, it is obvious that there are two ways of looking at any unit on the rankscale, upward or downward. If we look upward we are looking at how the unit operates in the structure of the unit next above; if we look downward we are looking at how the unit is made up by members of the unit next below. The former is called syntax and the latter is called morphology. Both syntax and morphology extend over the whole rankscale. The syntax of (for example) the nominal group is that it operates at s and c in clause structure; the

FIGURE 1

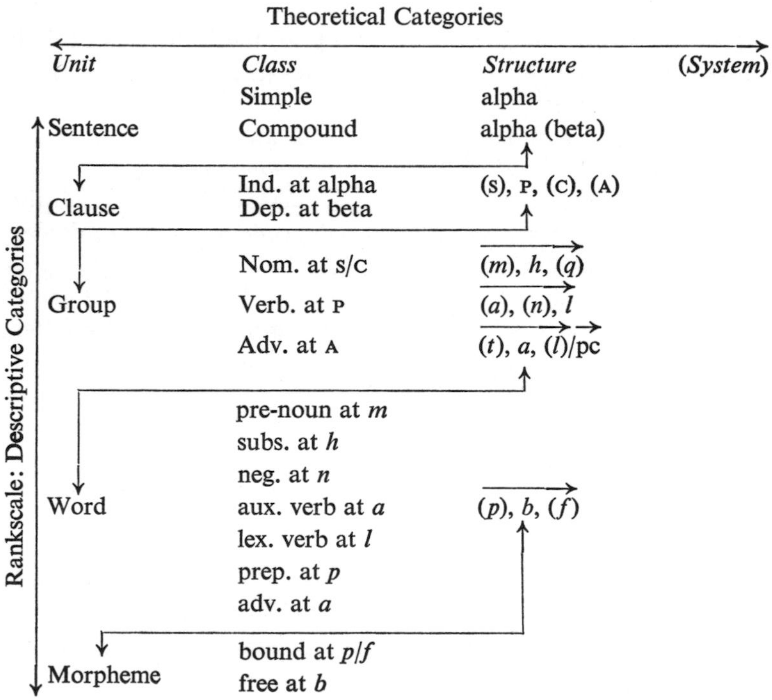

Theoretical Categories

Unit	Class	Structure	(System)
	Simple	alpha	
Sentence	Compound	alpha (beta)	
Clause	Ind. at alpha / Dep. at beta	(s), P, (c), (A)	
Group	Nom. at s/c	(m), h, (q)	
	Verb. at P	(a), (n), l	
	Adv. at A	(t), a, (l)/pc	
Word	pre-noun at m / subs. at h / neg. at n / aux. verb at a / lex. verb at l / prep. at p / adv. at a	(p), b, (f)	
Morpheme	bound at p/f / free at b		

Rankscale: Descriptive Categories

morphology of the nominal group is that it has elements of structure *m*, *h*, *q*, at which operate members of the unit word. Second, and consequent on the first point, we never, in fact, discuss only one unit on the rankscale; any discussion necessarily involves the unit next above or the unit next below.

Figure 1 is a diagrammatic presentation of what has been discussed; and (though perhaps somewhat forbidding at first) has proved useful as a mnemonic and as an illustration of the grammar here presented.

The following points may be noted:

(i) The arrowed lines connecting elements of structure and units indicate the syntactic ('upward') and the morphological ('downward') relationships discussed in the preceding paragraph.

(ii) Brackets round elements of structure indicate that these elements are optional, and are dependent on the presence of the obligatory element.

(iii) The arrowed lines above elements of structure indicate that the given sequence of elements is obligatory.

It will perhaps be advantageous at this point to introduce a shorthand for marking boundaries of units. The following symbols are used in this grammar:

Unit	Symbol	Example
Sentence	///	///The boys reminded Tom that he had hidden the books///
Clause	//	///The boys reminded Tom//that he had hidden the books///
Group	/	///The boys/reminded/Tom//that/he/ had hidden/the books///
Word		///The boys/reminded/Tom//that/he/ had hidden/the books///
Morpheme	+	///The boy+s/remind+ed/Tom//that/ he/had hid+(d)en/the book+s///

It follows from what has been said that the boundary of any unit will also be the boundary of all lower units. Thus, a sentence boundary is also a clause boundary, a group boundary, a word boundary and a morpheme boundary. The categories so far discussed will provide:

(i) a description of the units on the chain of linguistic events; this means naming patterned stretches on the linear succession of language activity;

(ii) class names for each of these units based on their place of operation in the chain;

(iii) a functional description based on the relations between classes of unit: e.g. *mh*, SP.

Thus we can analyse the sentence *the big dog will bite the little man in the arm* (stopping at group rank) as follows:

$\lessgtr$

α								
Ind								
S		P		C		A		
N		V		N		Ad		
m	*h*	*a*	*l*	*m*	*h*	*p*	C	
							m	*h*
The big	dog	will	bite	the little	man	in	the	arm

It should be noticed that each place on the chain provides an environment for further relations. Thus, s provides an environment for an *mh* relation, P provides an environment for an *al* relation, and so on.

Places on the chain also provide another sort of environment; not for further chain relations, but for choice relations. Choice here means the selection of one particular term at one particular place on the chain in preference to another term or other terms which are also possible at that place. Thus, at s we must have a nominal group as already discussed, but we have then to choose between singular and plural number; at P we must have a verbal group, but we have then to choose between present, past and future tense, and between positive and negative polarity, and between active and passive voice.

Sets of choices are in this way associated with places on the chain. Such a set of choices is called a system (the fourth of the theoretical categories), and the possible choices are terms or features of the system. Thus, there is a system of number, which has the terms singular and plural; and a system of tense, with the terms present, past and future. Diagrammatically:

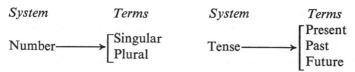

A network of such systems may be associated with a place on the chain. Some of these systems may depend on prior selection from other systems. In other words, some choices are more delicate choices than others, and the application of a scale of delicacy is important in the developing description of systems. The example of the number system is, in fact, an over-simplification. It is clear that at s in clause structure we may have a nominal group which chooses for number, or a nominal group which does not do so. Only if the former is chosen is there then the possibility of choosing between singular and plural. So these choices may be arranged according to delicacy in this way—

(See p. 120 *ff.*)

It is evident that grammar extends along two dimensions or axes. These have been informally designated 'chain' axis and 'choice' axis: a class denotes the potentiality of operation of a unit on the chain axis; a systemic term (or feature) denotes the selection made from a set of mutually exclusive choices at a place on the chain. In this book the expression 'Surface Grammar' denotes all that is implied by the former, and the expression 'Deep Grammar' all that is implied by the latter.

Chain and choice are presented diagrammatically in Figure 2.

FIGURE 2

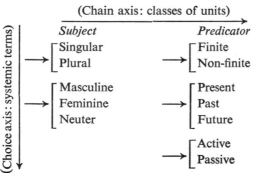

It is by way of systems that different syntagms (i.e. stretches of language which would be described differently on the chain axis) can be shown to be related, and similar syntagms (i.e. stretches of language which would be similarly described on the chain axis) can be shown to be unrelated. The two expressions (i) *Tom hit Bill* and (ii) *Bill was hit by Tom* will entail different surface descriptions. Thus:

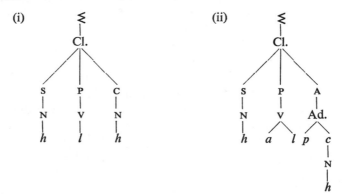

Conversely, the two expressions (iii) *The boy sings well* and (iv) *The material wears well* will entail similar surface descriptions. Thus:

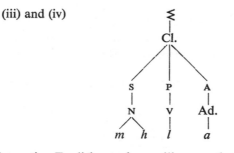

Yet native English speakers will agree that (i) and (ii) are grammatically related sentences, but (iii) and (iv) are not. If a grammar does not show that structurally dissimilar items may be closely related and that structurally similar items may be quite unrelated, then the grammar is inadequate as a description of how language works. The close grammatical relation of clauses (i) and (ii) is evident only in their deep grammar. The surface differences of these clauses can be attributed to the selection of different systemic terms. Thus, clause (i) has selected 'operative' and clause (ii) has selected 'receptive' from the system of transitivity.† It is clear that the surface grammar alone gives no direct indication of the grammatical relatedness of clauses. It can be further shown that the original expression

Tom hit Bill

is related to each of the expressions:

Bill was hit by Tom
Did Tom hit Bill?
It was Tom who hit Bill
Hit Bill, Tom.

by the selection of different systemic terms.

Some systems in English are discussed at length in Chapter 3. In the view of language presented here, the description of a language and items in a language requires two components—a surface component and a deep component. It is perhaps also obvious that as the description of grammar becomes more delicate we are approaching the problem of meaning; but, properly viewed, this is the direction from the beginning—it is not a question in language of 'grammar *and* meaning' but a question of 'grammatical meaning'.

† The significance of these terms, and their relation to surface structures is explained in section 3.1.4.

2
Surface Grammar

2.1 Morpheme and Word

It was stated in the General Survey that word was not the lowest unit in English grammar, but that a lower unit, the morpheme, operated at elements of structure of the word. The morpheme is formally established by comparing words and discovering recurrent patterns. Native English speakers will presumably agree that *hunting* is composed of two elements, *hunt* + *ing*, but that *stout* is not composed of two elements, *st* + *out*. This is so because the native speaker recognises the occurrence of patterns already evident in the language. He knows that *ing* appears after many other elements: *singing, shooting, swimming, turning, hoping* etc., and that *hunt* appears without other elements (i.e. as a word): tigers *hunt* their prey; the *hunt* was successful; and that 'hunt' also occurs before other endings: *hunts, hunted, hunter*. On the other hand, he knows that although *out* occurs alone and before other endings, *st* does not regularly occur with other items. He also knows that when *out* occurs alone it has a meaning that it does not have when it occurs as part of *stout*. Recognition of the various types of patterning requires a formulation and extended application of this intuitive process.

If we compare:

	eats	*eating*
with	*walks*	*walking*

or

	boy	*boys*
with	*lad*	*lads*

we can recognise identical stretches vertically and horizontally. We have, in fact, a 'square'[2] of the form

$$\begin{array}{|ll|}\hline AC & AD \\ BC & BD \\ \hline \end{array}$$

where A is *eat*, B is *walk*, C is *s* and D is *ing*. Such a procedure will provide a first step in the identification of morphemic structure of words.

There are some initial problems, however. First, it is obvious (since we can have structurally simple words) that there will be squares where one of the elements is represented by zero ($\emptyset$):

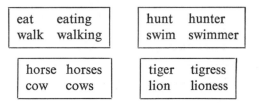

eat	eating	hunt	hunter
walk	walking	swim	swimmer

horse	horses	tiger	tigress
cow	cows	lion	lioness

In the interest of methodological consistency we can say that a word such as *eat* is composed of an element expounded by *eat* and an element expounded by $\emptyset$: but this is only a methodological convenience which enables us to utilise the principle of the square. The convention will be dropped in the final description of word structure.

A second problem is that we intuitively want to include such pairs as *man*:*men goose*:*geese sheep*:*sheep*. The intuition is consolidated by formal considerations. We are concerned in this chapter primarily with the morpheme, but also with the word since (as discussed in the General Survey) we are always concerned with two units on the rank-scale. If we look at the syntax of the word we find that the *man*:*men* type pattern in the same way as *boy*:*boys*. This means that they will conform to the criteria for 'noun' (p. 27) and carry distinctions of number and case (pp. 120, 123). It may also be said that we know (or can elicit from a native speaker) that *men* means 'more than one man' just as *boys* means 'more than one boy'. Such semantic evidence may be accepted as corroboration, but it is the overall syntactic patterning which is criterial. In short, the following frames—

The . . . is coming   *The . . . are coming*
     boy   boys
     man   men
     goose   geese
     sheep   sheep

will accommodate only one member of each pair. In terms of our square we can formalise this by stating that if we have a pair of words which are syntactically and semantically like other pair(s), as *man:men* is to *boy:boys*, then the first pair is acceptable if the second pair enters into a perfect square, as

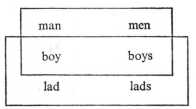

A third problem is encountered by the occurrence of squares such as

detain	contain
deceive	conceive.

In such squares our analysis will yield the items *de, tain, ceive, con* as elements of structure of words. None of these items, however, occur alone as do the items *boy, lad, man, walk,* etc. If we recognise such squares we must qualify this by saying that the elements of such words are different from the elements of other words; in fact, we have a small number of base elements which are bound (do not occur alone) in contrast to the vast majority of base elements which are free (which do occur alone). Again we find semantic corroboration in that we cannot attach meanings to the elements *tain, ceive,* etc. as we can with *s* (plural) or *ed* (past) or *er* (agent).

We can, then, identify a word as simple or complex in structure, as composed of one morpheme (if it has ∅ in the square) or more than one morpheme, if it enters into a square of one of the following types:

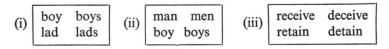

The element which is common horizontally we will call the base element of structure—and dispense with the $\emptyset$ conventions, so that *boy* does not analyse as base $+ \emptyset$ but rather as base; the element which is common vertically we will call affix, and further distinguish as prefix (p) and postfix (f) according to whether they precede or follow the base.

This yields the elements of structure of the word pbf; since it can be seen that b may occur alone, but that p and f only occur in association with a b, we can more delicately represent elements of structure of the word

$$\overrightarrow{(p), b, (f)}$$

where brackets indicate optional elements of structure; the arrow indicates that these elements, when occurring, must occur in this sequence, and the commas indicate that this is a list of elements of structure (not a structure; we can only have a structure of a given unit).

The vast majority of base elements in English are realised by one free morpheme, e.g. *boy*, *lad*, *horse*, *cow*, *mountain*, *sky*. There are, however, bases such as *bookcase*, *blackbird*, which enter into squares—

bookcase	bookcases
boy	boys

That is, we shall have structures such as *bf* where *b* is realised by an item such as *bookcase*. But *book* and *case* are themselves established as free morphemes operating as base elements in word structure. We may call this b_2 as distinguished from the mono-morphemic base (b_1). Still another type of base must be accounted for: the type exemplified by *tain* and *ceive* above. We may call this b_3. We thus have:

b_1 a structurally simple base realised by one free morpheme.

b_2 a structurally compound base realised by two free morphemes (*bookcase*, *sandstone*).

b_3 a structurally compound base realised by two bound morphemes (*deceive*, *detain*).

We have morphemes which can occur alone, classed as free; and morphemes which cannot occur alone, classed as bound. Free morphemes operate at b_1 and b_2; bound morphemes operate at b_3 and at p and f.

A further consideration of word structure will show that there are two main classes of bound morphemes. One class will form into morphological paradigms or sets; e.g.

(i) *eat, eats, ate, eating, eaten*
(ii) *boy, boy's, boys, boys'*
(iii) *green, greener, greenest.*

The morphemes occurring in such sets are called inflexional morphemes, and are distinguished from bound morphemes which do not enter into such sets; e.g.

$$\left.\begin{array}{l}\textit{-ish}\\ \textit{-ist}\\ \textit{-ise}\end{array}\right\} \text{ as in } \left\{\begin{array}{l}\textit{boyish}\\ \textit{novelist}\\ \textit{normalise.}\end{array}\right.$$

This second class of morphemes are called derivational morphemes. In addition to forming morphological sets, inflexional morphemes

(i) are not recursive; only one inflexional morpheme may occur in the structure of any one word,
(ii) such an inflexional morpheme always occurs finally in word structure, and therefore
(iii) if both a derivational and an inflexional morpheme occur in the structure of a word, then the derivational morpheme must precede the inflexional morpheme, e.g. *novel* + *ist* + *s*.

Derivational morphemes, on the other hand,

(i) may be recursive, e.g. *boy* + *ish* + *ness* (but sequences are fixed, we cannot have **boy* + *ness* + *ish*);
(ii) do not form morphological sets; and so cannot be fully accounted for in grammar; they may be considered as on the border of grammar and lexis;
(iii) if a derivational and an inflexional morpheme are present in the structure of a word, then the derivational morpheme must be non-final as noted above.

2.1.1 *Inflexion*

It is obvious that the three types of morphological sets above correspond to the traditional word-classes of verb, noun, adjective. It must be stressed again that classes of units are determined syntactically, not morphologically; thus, *boy* will be classed as a noun because it patterns in a certain way in syntax (to be described in the next chapter), not because it enters into the morphological pattern discussed above. It is because of this that we class *sheep* also as a noun which enters into singular and plural contrast though it is structurally dissimilar to *boy*. This, of course, is why we included the *man*:*men*/*child*:*children* type in the squares. Nevertheless, though syntactic criteria take precedence over morphological criteria, if there is some congruence between syntactic and morphological criteria in a language then this is helpful and can be utilised in description. In English there is considerable congruence between syntactically defined classes of noun, verb, adjective and the morphological sets discussed above. Thus we can say that:

> *boy boy's boys boys'*
> *eat eats ate eating eaten*
> *green greener greenest*

form a typical noun, verb and adjective paradigm respectively.

Before discussing English inflexions in more detail, it is necessary to discuss the relations between the morpheme, or more properly the morpheme class, and its realisation in substance. Anticipating the material of a future chapter (p. 120), we can say that the word-class noun is involved in selection from the system of number, which has the terms singular and plural. If we say that *boy* is a typical example of noun singular and that *boys* is a typical example of noun plural, it might appear that we are saying that the written ⟨s⟩ or the spoken /z/ *is* the morpheme plural. But formal units are not the same as the substance by which they are realised. The ⟨s⟩ and /z/ are examples of how the morpheme plural may be realised, but they are not the morpheme plural. The morpheme plural, in fact, has no 'shape'; it, like other units, is an abstraction from the linguistic data. Grammar is concerned with classes of items, not with particular realisations in substance. The grammatical analysis of *boys* is noun:plural and of *men* is noun:plural. That the former is formed by adding ⟨s⟩ or /z/ to the singular but the latter is not formed in this way does not affect the grammatical classification.

The morpheme class plural has various realisations, among which are vowel alternation *man*:*men*, and no overt change from the singular form *sheep*:*sheep* (i.e. no change morphologically; we could say plurality is realised by concord with determiners and verbs: *this sheep is*:*those sheep are*; see further p. 120 *ff.*).

NOUN INFLEXION

The vast majority of English nouns do form the plural by adding a substantial realisation of the plural morpheme to the singular form. In spelling, this means the addition of ⟨(e)s⟩ (though syllabic ⟨y⟩ is replaced by ⟨i⟩ *lady*:*ladies*, and ⟨f⟩ may alternate with ⟨v⟩); in pronunciation the realisation is various.

1. After the fricatives /s, z/ and the affricates /t, d/ the addition is /Iz/:

Singular	Plural		
price	⟨s⟩	/Iz/	*prices*
judge	⟨s⟩	/Iz/	*judges*
church	⟨es⟩	/Iz/	*churches*
maze	⟨s⟩	/Iz/	*mazes*

2. After /p, f, t/ the addition is /s/:

Singular	Plural		
cap	⟨s⟩	/s/	*caps*
laugh	⟨s⟩	/s/	*laughs*
cut	⟨s⟩	/s/	*cuts*

3. After /n, m, b, d/ the addition is /z/:

Singular	Plural		
bun	⟨s⟩	/z/	*buns*
sum	⟨s⟩	/z/	*sums*
ring	⟨s⟩	/z/	*rings*
cub	⟨s⟩	/z/	*cubs*
wood	⟨s⟩	/z/	*woods*

4. In some nouns the plural form involves the change of a voiceless fricative to a voiced fricative and the addition of /z/ or in (c) below /Iz/:

(a) /f/ becomes /v/ and /z/ is added; in spelling this requires the replacing of ⟨f⟩ by ⟨v⟩ and the addition of ⟨es⟩:

Singular	Plural		
calf	⟨f→v⟩ + ⟨es⟩	/f/→/v/ + /z/	*calves*
elf	⟨f→v⟩ + ⟨es⟩	/f/→/v/ + /z/	*elves*
wolf	⟨f→v⟩ + ⟨es⟩	/f/→/v/ + /z/	*wolves*

Thus: *half, knife, leaf, life, loaf, scarf, sheaf, shelf, thief, wife.*

(b) /θ/ becomes /ð/ and /z/ is added; in spelling this requires only the addition of ⟨s⟩:

Singular	Plural	
path	$/\theta/\rightarrow/\eth/ + /z/$	*paths*

(c) /s/ becomes /z/ and /Iz/ is added; in spelling only the addition of ⟨s⟩.

Singular	Plural	
house	⟨s⟩ $/s/\rightarrow/z/ + /Iz/$	*houses*

5. In some nouns no addition is involved, but there is an associated vowel change; the sound change requires the corresponding spelling change:

Singular	Plural
man	*men*
foot	*feet*
tooth	*teeth*
goose	*geese*
louse	*lice*
mouse	*mice*
woman	*women*
penny	*pence*

6. Plurals of foreign nouns show considerable variation, and nearly all such will, in some varieties of speech, occur as 'Anglicised' plurals:

Singular	Plural
nebula	*nebulae*
datum	*data*
criterion	*criteria*
phenomenon	*phenomena*
crisis	*crises*

7. The 'double plural' *children* involves vowel change from the singular and the addition of /rən/; and the plural *oxen* involves the addition of /ən/:

Singular	Plural
child	*children*
ox	*oxen*

English nouns are also inflected for marked case (p. 123 *ff.*). This requires the addition of /s, z, Iz/ to the singular and plural forms; which particular phoneme occurs depends on the preceding phoneme (as in plural formation). In spelling, this requires the addition of ⟨'s⟩ to the singular and ⟨s'⟩ to the plural.

ADJECTIVE INFLEXION

There is a theoretical problem in classing adjective morphemes as inflexional or derivational; they partake of the characteristics of both. Though they are here being classed as inflexional, which is perhaps the conventional view, this is only a convenience of description. The problem should be appreciated.

There is no problem concerning the structure of adjectives: the positive form consists of a base, the comparative and superlative of base + postfix (bf):

b	b	p	b	p
green	*green* + *er*	*green* + *est*.		

They appear to be inflexions, and perhaps most of us would class them as such intuitively. This is because, like noun and verb inflexions, they form a restricted set; they do not have the variety exhibited by derivational endings; they help to identify a major word-class. Against this, however, there are three arguments:

(i) They do not enter into concord relations, a relationship relevant to nouns and verbs. In the expressions

the big boy walks: *the big boys walk*

the noun and verb show morphological change, but the adjective does not.

(ii) Although they help to identify a major word-class, they in fact only identify a number of members of this class. Many adjectives form their comparative and superlative periphrastically by preposing *more* and *most*.

(iii) Some of their members can be followed by inflectional morphemes: *our elders, our betters*.

The adjectives which regularly form the comparative and superlative by adding -er, -est are of three types:

(i) practically all monosyllabic adjectives:

 green, bright, fast, soft, fine, etc.

(ii) disyllabic adjective which end in -ly, -le, -er, -ow:

 holy, noble, clever, shallow

(iii) a few other disyllabic adjectives:

 common, concise, cruel, obscure, profound, quiet.

Longer adjectives usually prepose *more* and *most*; but it should be noted that adjectives which regularly have -er, -est can also prepose *more, most.* There are a few irregular adjectives in English, forming their comparative and superlative by suppletion:

good	*better*	*best*
bad	*worse*	*worst*
little	*less*	*least*
much	*more*	*most*

VERB INFLEXION

The verb is that word-class which operates in the verbal group; this primary class is subdivided into two secondary classes, auxiliary verbs and lexical verbs (pp. 41 *ff.*). Lexical verbs have from three to five different forms; because of syntactic patterning it is necessary to recognise five forms as 'forms of the verb': these may be illustrated by:

eat eats ate eating eaten.

For convenience, these forms will be referred to in this book as the

base -s -ed -ing -en

form of the verb respectively. Not all verbs distinguish five forms morphologically, and it is only because some members of the class do have five forms that invariable forms in other verbs can in fact be recognised as different syntactic forms. The variant forms of the verb can be realised by linear addition, as always with the -s form and the -ing form:

base	-s	-ing
walk	*walks*	*walking*
run	*runs*	*running.*

The -d form may be realised by addition of a plosive consonant to the base form, or by vowel alternation in the base form, or by both vowel change in the base form and addition of a plosive consonant:

base	-d	(change/addition)	
walk	*walked*	$+\langle ed \rangle$ $+/t/$	
take	*took*	$\langle a \rangle \rightarrow \langle oo \rangle$	$/ei/ \rightarrow /u/.$
say	*said*	$\langle a \rangle \rightarrow \langle ai \rangle$	$/ei/ \rightarrow /\varepsilon/.$

The verb may be what is usually called 'invariable', i.e. may not morphologically distinguish between the base and the -d form—

base	-d	-en
cut	*cut*	*cut*
hit	*hit*	*hit.*

It is evident that these 'invariable' verbs do not distinguish the -en form morphologically from the base and -d forms; most English

C

verbs, in fact, do not morphologically distinguish between the -d
and -en forms:

-d	-en
loved	*loved*
walked	*walked*
said	*said.*

The -en form is sometimes marked by addition of ⟨en⟩, /en/;
sometimes the -en form has the same vowel as the base and sometimes
the same vowel as the -d form, but sometimes it has a different vowel
from either.

PERSONAL PRONOUNS

Personal pronouns have separate forms for distinguishing terms in a
system of person (1st, 2nd, 3rd person) and, for the 3rd person
singular, terms in a system of gender (masculine, feminine, neuter;
see p. 127); they also distinguish terms in a system of case (s-case,
non s-case; and terms in a system of number (singular, plural; see
see pp. 120 *ff*). This is shown in tabular form in Figure 3.

FIGURE 3

		Singular			Plural		
		s-case	Non s-case	Gen.	s-case	Non s-case	Gen.
1st Person		I	me	my/mine	we	us	our(s)
2nd Person		you	you	your(s)	you	you	your(s)
3rd Person	m.	he	him	his	they	them	their(s)
	f.	she	her	her(s)			
	n.	it	it	its			

The alternative forms of the genitives indicate that the form without
the ⟨s⟩ (and *my*) occurs when the item operates at *d* in nominal
group structure, and the form with the ⟨s⟩ (and *mine*) occurs when
the item operates at *h* in nominal group structure (at c). Thus:

It is her book   *This book is hers.*
It is my book   *This book is mine.*

2.2 *Word and Group*

The previous chapter was concerned with the syntax of the morpheme and the morphology of the word. This chapter takes one step up the rankscale, and is concerned with the syntax of the word and the morphology of the group. Any discussion of group structure must take account of the different classes of group in English. It is the case that the units word, clause and sentence have classes which are similar enough for these units to be assigned basic structures irrespective of their various classes; thus in the previous chapter the structure of the unit word (irrespective of classes such as noun, verb, etc.) could be generalised as (p), b, (f). The different classes of the unit group do not have enough in common to admit of such a generalisation in respect of structure.

In the clause, *the big dog will bite the little man in the arm/deeply* there are four elements of structure:

1	2	3	4

(the big dog) (will bite) (the little man) (in the arm/deeply)

To these elements of structure we can give the well-established names subject (s), predicator (p), complement (c), adjunct (a). It is evident that in clause structure the patterns at the elements 1 and 3 above (i.e. s and c) are alike. Thus, though there are four elements of structure, we require only three classes of group defined syntactically, since one class of group operates at two places in clause structure. Accordingly, the following three classes of group are established:

nominal group (operating at s/c in clause structure)
verbal group (operating at p in clause structure)
adverbial group (operating at a in clause structure).

The elements of structure of these groups, and the word-classes operating at these elements are discussed in the following sections.

2.2.1 *Nominal Group*[3]

In the structure of the nominal group there is an obligatory element; this is called the head or headword. The simplest type of nominal group is therefore one which consists of an *h* element which is realised by one word, as the italicised items in the following:

Cows eat *grass.*	*Fish* swim.
He was *pale.*	*John* shot *Jim.*
Mountains are *magnificent.*	*Cowboys* chase *horses.*

The *h* element may be preceded by another element; this is called the modifier (*m*), and though this element may be realised by a number of words (as any element may be) they are primarily grouped together as realising the element *m*. The following groups have the structure *mh*:

$$
\begin{array}{c|c}
m & h \\
the & boy
\end{array}
$$

$$
\begin{array}{c|c}
m & h \\
the\ big & boy
\end{array}
$$

$$
\begin{array}{c|c}
m & h \\
the\ very\ big & boy
\end{array}
$$

$$
\begin{array}{c|c}
m & h \\
all\ the\ other\ big\ American & boys
\end{array}
$$

There is also an element of structure which may follow the *h* element; this is called the qualifier (*q*). The following groups have the structure *hq*:

$$
\begin{array}{c|c}
h & q \\
Boys & with\ red\ hair\ (are\ nice)
\end{array}
$$

$$
\begin{array}{c|c}
h & q \\
Houses & in\ the\ country\ (were\ fashionable\ then)
\end{array}
$$

$$
\begin{array}{c|c}
h & q \\
Cars & that\ break\ down\ (are\ a\ nuisance)
\end{array}
$$

All three elements may, of course, be present; the following groups have the structure *mhq*:

$$
\begin{array}{c|c|c}
m & h & q \\
The\ big & boy & with\ red\ hair\ (scored\ the\ first\ goal)
\end{array}
$$

$$
\begin{array}{c|c|c}
m & h & q \\
The\ old & car & that\ I\ sold\ (is\ still\ going\ strong)
\end{array}
$$

$$
\begin{array}{c|c|c}
m & h & q \\
(He\ bought)\ a\ nice & house & in\ the\ country
\end{array}
$$

The elements *m*, *h*, *q*, are the elements of structure whose particular configuration (*h*; *mh*; *hq*; *mhq*) will form the structure of any given nominal group. Since *h* is an obligatory element, but *m* and *q* are optional and dependent, we may list the primary elements of structure of the nominal group as:

$$
\overrightarrow{(m),\ h,\ (q)}
$$

where, as previously, the arrow indicates that sequence is invariable, the brackets indicate optional elements, and the commas indicate that this is a list of elements of structure, not a structure.

It is perhaps worth repeating that primary structure brings together all those items which share a potentiality of occurrence. Thus a complex nominal group such as:

all the other ten very worn school books in the library

and a relatively simple group such as:

the man himself

are both analysed primarily as *mhq*:

$$m \qquad\qquad\qquad\qquad h \qquad q$$

all the other ten very worn school | *books* | *in the library*

$$m \quad\mid\quad h \quad\mid\quad q$$

the | *man* | *himself.*

A headword can thus have a modifier preceding it and/or a qualifier following it. Some headwords occur with a considerable variety of modifiers and qualifiers, but others do not. The words which operate at *h* in nominal group structure may be classified according to the patternings of modifier and qualifier with which they occur.

Since it is possible to have simple nominal groups, i.e. groups with only a headword, it is obvious that we can first of all class together all those words which can appear at *h*. We can call this class substantive, and the words operating at *h* in the minimal nominal groups in the following are therefore substantives:

Horses run *races*.   *I* live in *Glasgow*.   *Running* is *fun*.
Training is *good* for *you*.   *He* sings *songs*.

If headwords in more complex groups are considered it becomes obvious that different members of the class substantive occur in different patterns. There are four main subclasses.

(i)

$$h \qquad\qquad\qquad h$$

These boys are *superb examples*.

$$h$$

The bath I had was very refreshing.

$$h \qquad\qquad\qquad\qquad\qquad\qquad h$$

All the books that I read on holiday belonged to *my brother*.

$$h$$

The spot where the river bends is tricky to negotiate.

The words operating at *h* in the italicised groups are nouns. The positive characteristics of the word-class noun are that its members occur with a large variety of modifiers and qualifiers (demonstratives, adjectives and, in particular, the definite and indefinite articles), and they exhibit the morphology discussed in the preceding chapter. Negatively, they are characterised by the fact that they cannot be modified by the submodifiers *very, rather, quite.*

(ii)

        h   *h*
Nobody in the room would admit to *it.*
       h   *h*
She danced *me* off my feet.
       h   *h*
Anyone who is an artist will tell *you.*
       h
They all went up the hill.
       h
They both play very well.

The words which operate at *h* in the italicised groups are pronouns. Pronouns are not usually modified, though they can be qualified. The qualifiers of pronouns are themselves complete clauses or groups of somewhat restricted types, as in:

       h   *q*
Anyone [*who is an artist*]
       h   *q*
Nobody [*in the room*].

Some pronouns occur uniquely with other qualifiers:

(a) the so-called 'indefinite pronouns' occur with the item 'else'—

       h   *q*

everyone ⎫
no one   ⎪
someone ⎬ else
somebody ⎪
nobody   ⎭

(b) the 'plural personal pronouns' occur with the item 'both'—

       h   *q*

they ⎫ both
we   ⎭

Pronouns, then, take virtually no modifiers, and restricted qualifiers; in this they differ from nouns. In particular, they cannot be modified by the definite or indefinite article.

(iii)

    h

London is the capital.

          h

Come to *Canada*.

    h   *h*

Matthews won the cup for *Blackpool*.

The words operating at *h* in the italicised groups are proper nouns. Proper nouns cannot be modified or qualified, and so differ from other types of headword. The occurrence of groups such as *Bonnie Scotland, Sunny Sussex*, does not invalidate this statement. The adjectives in such groups clearly do not fulfill the usual function of adjectives in the nominal group. They do not identify the headword as a particular member of its class: thus, *dark night* means 'of the class *night* that member which is characterised by *darkness*', or *sunny day* means 'a day which is sunny'; but *Sunny Sussex* does not mean 'of the class Sussex that member which is *sunny*; a *Sussex* which is *sunny*'.

(iv)

      h

He was *old*.

               h

His attempt was *rather feeble*.

            h

She turned *quite pale* at this.

The words operating at *h* in the italicised groups are adjectives. They have a restricted range of modifiers and qualifiers; they can be qualified by the items *enough, indeed*, or by complete clauses or groups of restricted types:

      h   *q*

He is *older* [*than Harry*]

      h   *q*

He is *keener* ⟦*than I am*⟧

        m h   *q*

He kept himself *as fit* [*as possible*].

Unlike nouns, adjectives cannot be modified by articles or demonstratives; but they can be modified by the submodifiers *very, rather, quite*, etc.

These various characteristics are intended as formal definitions of the word-classes noun, pronoun, proper noun, adjective, as opposed to the semantic definitions of the type 'a noun is the name of a place, person or thing, living or dead'.

The structure of nominal groups which have a noun at h are the most varied and complex, which is what we should expect since noun is defined as that type of headword occurring with more types of m and q than other types of headword. So that, although the complex group *all the other ten very worn American school books in the house* may be primarily analysed as *mhq*, it is apparent that the occurrence of the various items is not random, that there are, in fact, discernible secondary structures at m. Sequence of items is important, since we can have:

    all houses
    all the houses
    all the same houses

but not:

    *the all houses/same all the houses
    *all houses the/ten the houses
    *stone the five all houses same.

The more we disturb the sequence the more unacceptable the group becomes. On the basis of this obligatory sequence we can establish secondary elements of structure at m. Thus:

d	o	e	n	(h)
all the other	*ten*	*very worn American*	*school*	*(books)*

The names for these secondary elements of structure are:

- d deictic (at which operates the word-class determiner)
- n numerative (at which operates the word-class numeral)
- e epithet (at which operates the word-class adjective)
- c classifier (at which operates the same word-class as at h).

Looking more closely at the element d, we find that there are further sequence restrictions within this:

we may have {all the other / both the same}

but not * {the all other / the same both / other the all / same the both.}

We have, in fact, three distinct places at d:

d^1 (predeictic)   *all, both, half*
d^2 (deictic)   *the, this, that*; *his, its, John's, mother's, my*; *a, any, another, no, neither, every, several*
d^3 (post-deictic)   *other, same.*

The occurrence of items at d is not entirely independent of other items at m, as might appear from the segmentation of m given above. The occurrence of items at d is related to the occurrence of items at o. At o the two types of numerals operate (cardinal and ordinal). When we use cardinal numerals they can be selected independently of *determiners*. Groups such as—

   one horse   five horses   the five horses   the same five horses

show that such numerals may occur with or without a determiner. It should be noted, however, that number concord is required between numerals and headwords; i.e. the cardinal *one* requires a singular headword, and other cardinals require a plural headword. When we use ordinal numerals we require a determiner for 'identifying'. Thus:

his first opportunity	*his first attempts*
John's third bicycle	*her third trials*
my ninth birthday	*their ninth birthdays*

These examples show that ordinal numerals require a determiner, but also that they do not require number concord with the headword, since the same numerals occur in the second column with plural headwords as occurred in the first column with singular headwords.

At the element e the word-class adjective operates (it has already been shown that this class can operate at h also), and the number of items in this class is very great. At this element of structure in the nominal group recursion becomes marked; that is, there are often two or more exponents of e present in one group. The position at e is somewhat more complicated than at d, and the place orderings, the permissible sequences, have not been fully worked out. The sequences are not invariable, they are preferred rather than prescribed, and even the usual sequences can be altered if accompanied by an intonation break. There is, however, a general pattern which gives fairly clear guidance. Adjectives which identify the headword by 'comparison' or 'degree' seem to occur in first position; this means adjectives which are regularly compared either by preposing *more*:*most* or taking the -er:-est inflexions, and adjectives which are submodified by items such as *rather, quite, very, terribly, unbearably,* etc. We may call this position e^1. Thus:

$$e^1 \qquad\qquad e^1$$
the ten nicest men   a very lovely landscape
$$e^1 \qquad\qquad e^1$$
the cleverer brown dog   the rather elegant man
$$e^1 \qquad\qquad e^1$$
the more graceful blue car   the oldest wooden houses
$$e^1$$
the fifteen best American sprinters

It can be seen from these examples that such adjectives precede other adjectives such as *blue, American, wooden.* It can also be seen that there are two points to note when superlative adjectives occur at e^1: i) the presence of a superlative in this position requires a determiner at d, a relation similar to that obtaining between ordinal numerals and determiners. Thus:

the best chair   his most polished performance   the sheerest silk

and ii) a superlative almost always points forward to a q in the nominal group. Thus:

$$e^1 \quad h \qquad q \qquad\qquad e^1 \quad h \qquad q$$
the best chair [in the room]   the most graceful animal [in the world]

Place orderings within e^1 itself can be distinguished. In first place occurs the 'size-shape' group, in second place the 'quality' group, in third place the 'age' group. Thus:

size	shape	quality	age
big	fat	fine	young
tall	thin	graceful	old
large	slim	scraggy	new
huge	square	precious	year-old
etc.	etc.	etc.	etc.

We rarely have groups with a member from each group present, but smaller groupings suggest this sequence. That is, we find:

the tall scraggy man   rather than   *the scraggy tall man*
a large square object   „   „   *a square large object*
a tall young man   „   „   *a young tall man*
a precious young thing   „   „   *a young precious thing.*

These adjectives are followed (at e^2) by the 'colour' adjectives. The colour adjectives are less readily submodified, and have a range of submodifiers with which they typically occur. Thus:

> *salmon pink   emerald green   royal blue   dark blue*
> *bottle green   buttercup yellow*

These adjectives are followed in turn (at e^3) by what may be called the derived adjectives such as *wooden, silken, American, strategic,* etc. That is, adjectives formally derived from other word-classes, so they are usually compound in structure. These adjectives do not regularly take comparison. Thus:

$$e^1 \quad e^2 \quad e^3 \qquad\qquad e^1 \quad e^1 \quad e^3$$
> *the large blue American carpet   the huge old wooden trunk*

At the element *n* operates the same word-class as operates at *h* in the nominal group. It is often said that a noun in this position is 'acting as an adjective', and should presumably be considered as an exponent of *e*. There are, however, both formal and semantic differences between adjectives at *m* and nouns at *m*. In the most general terms, items which operate at *e* denote accidental properties of the headword, but items which operate at *n* denote inherent properties of the headword: thus, *a stony path* is not the same as *a stone path*; *a stony path* is presumably a path which has stones on or in it, but this is not an essential feature and does not contribute to the inherent nature of the path; *a stone path*, on the other hand, is presumably a path made of stone, and the 'stoneness' is an inherent property of the path. Formally, *stony* may be compared like other adjectives, but *stone* may not; it is possible (if unlikely) that *a stony stone path* may occur, but not *a stone stony path*.

Since both *n* and *h* are expounded by the same word-class, and since both may be compound, there is potential ambiguity in identifying structures. This type of nominal group, frequently with several exponents of *n*, is now well-developed in English and is a feature of the present-day language in some registers. Intonation is important in the spoken language for identifying such structures, and hyphenation in the written language, though there is no great consistency in the written language in this respect.

The essential characteristic of *h* in a nominal group is that it contains the final stressed syllable, as in (stressed syllable italicised):

> the white *house*
> the black *bird*   structure: *deh*
> the old *book*

Compound headwords can therefore be identified by the fact that their first base element will contain a stressed syllable, final in the group, but their second element will not, as in:

the *White*house
the *black*bird   structure: *dh* (*h* compound)
his *pocket*-book

Nominal groups which have a structure *nh* will normally have a stressed syllable on the *n* element and on the *h* element. This means, of course, that *h* is still identifiable as the final stressed syllable. Thus:

the *coin boxes*
the *hotel prices*   structure: *dnh*
the *gold mine*
the *passenger vehicles*

Difficulty of interpretation may arise either when there is more than one exponent of *n*, or when there is a structure *nh* in which one or the other exponent is compound. The main types are listed below, and hyphenation is consistently used to indicate compound items though in some of the (occurring) examples hyphenation was not present.

(i)

> *time-table commitments*
> *bank-rate rise*
> *man-hole cover*

The structure of these groups is *nh* (*n* compound). Normally such groups will contain a stressed syllable on the first base element of *n* and have an intonation break (//) between *n* and *h*. Thus:

time-table//com*mit*ments
bank-rate//*rise*
man-hole//*co*ver

(ii)

> *school sum-book*
> *London road-map*
> *roadside telephone-boxes*

The structure of these groups is *nh* (*h* compound). Normally such groups will contain a stressed syllable on *n* and a stressed syllable on the first base element of *h*, and have an intonation break between *n* and *h*. Thus:

school//*sum*-book
*Lon*don//*road*-map
*road*side//*tel*ephone-boxes

(iii)

subscriber trunk dialling
Fife County Council
London briar pipes

The structure of these groups is *nnh*. This structure is perhaps less common than the preceding two. They are by no means unusual, however; and they may have several exponents of *n*: consider—

subscriber trunk dialling
subscriber trunk dialling system
subscriber trunk dialling all-number system
subscriber trunk dialling all-number system fault
subscriber trunk dialling all-number system fault engineer

Structural ambiguity seems highly possible, but in practice the context of the utterance is usually such that only one interpretation is possible. (*Cf. a head buyer* (i) in Glasgow, (ii) in Borneo: suggest different structures!) Nevertheless, the decision between assigning the structure *nnh* and *nh* (with one or the other compound) may on occasions be difficult and perhaps arbitrary.

In general, a different type of item occurs at *q* than that which occurs at *m*. The element *q* is typically realised by a complete group or clause. That is, another complete unit operates as an element of structure in the nominal group, a unit of the same or higher rank. For example, in the clause, *the man I visited in town has gone away* the subject is *the man I visited in town*. It has already been said that the element subject is realised by a nominal group. It is obvious, however, that this example consists of not just one group, but several; and indeed the organisation of only part of this sequence is what we shall find in clause structure. We can, in other words, morphologically identify *I visited in town* as a clause: it has a structure SPA.

A clause normally operates higher on the rankscale, in the structure of the sentence; indeed, this is crucial in the definition of clause. In the present example, therefore, this clause seems to have moved down the rankscale in order to operate in the less usual position of *q* in a nominal group. Since the grammar is concerned with the arrangement of units on a rankscale, a clause operating in the structure of a lower unit is said to be rankshifted. The use of this term is a descriptive convenience; the structure could easily be called something else (the traditional terms 'restricted/non-restricted', 'defining/non-defining' would describe relative clauses so involved, but there are a few other rankshifts in English, and a generic term is needed). The main point is that such structures have to be accounted for.

It is important to distinguish between clauses which are operating in sentence structure (the norm; not rankshifted) and clauses which are operating at *q* in the nominal group (rankshifted). In the clauses:

> *the man who came to dinner stayed a month*
> *nobody who calls himself an artist would paint like that*

the nominal groups operating at s have rankshifted clauses at *q*:

	S		
	N		
m	*h*	*q*	
The	man	⟦who came to dinner⟧	stayed a month

S		
N		
h	*q*	
Nobody	⟦who calls himself an artist⟧	would paint like that.

In:

> *My dad, who is an artist, paints pictures like that*
> *The American runner, who was getting on a bit, failed to finish.*

the clauses are operating in sentence structure. In the written language such clauses are marked off by commas, and in the spoken language they are marked off by intonation breaks.

Also at *q*, as is evident from earlier examples, other complete groups operate. The normal place of operation of groups is in clause structure, so groups operating within the structure of another group are also called rankshifted. In the clauses:

> *a car that price is beyond me*
> *shoes this size are usually dearer*

the nominal groups operating at s have rankshifted nominal groups at *q*. Thus:

	S	
	N	
m	*h*	*q*
A	*car*	[that price] is beyond me

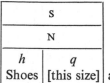

S	
N	
h	*q*
Shoes	[this size]

Shoes [this size] are usually dearer.

It is very common for adverbial groups to operate at *q* in nominal group structure, rather than their normal operation at A in clause structure. In the clauses:

I bought a house in the city
the snow on the hill was deep
he chose the books with leather bindings

the nominal groups: *a house in the city, the snow on the hill, the books with leather bindings* have adverbial groups operating at *q*. Thus:

S		
N		
m	*h*	*q*
The	snow	[on the hill]

The snow [on the hill] was deep

C		
N		
m	*h*	*q*
the	books	[with leather bindings]

He chose the books [with leather bindings].

Complexity at *q* is occasioned mainly by recursion. In most instances this is a relation of successive rankshifting: there is one *q* in the group but this *q* itself has a structure which contains further rank-shifts. Thus, *I found him in the house in the main street* does not mean *I found him (a) in the house, and (b) in the main street,* but rather *I found him in the house* (i.e. *the house which*) *is in the main street.* The analysis is therefore:

S	P	C	A			
N	V	N	Ad			
h	*l*	*h*	*p*	C = [N]		
				m	*h*	*q*
I	found	him	in	[the	house	[in the main street.]]

Such sequences can become quite complex. If we add *in the town* to the above example we will have a further *rankshift*. And, although most examples can be successively analysed as above, there are occasions when there is ambiguity between successive adjuncts in clause structure and rankshifted adverbial groups at *q* in nominal group structure. For example, if, *he decided on the house in the country* means *he decided on the house which was in the country*, then the clause has a structure SPC, and C is realised by a nominal group which has a rankshifted adverbial group at *q*:

S	P	C		
N	V	N		
h	*l*	*m*	*h*	*q*
He	*decided on*	*the*	*house*	*[in the country.]*

If, however, it means *while in the country he made up his mind about the house* then there is an adjunct in the clause structure:

S	P	C		A		
N	V	N		Ad		
h	*l*	*m*	*h*	*p*	C = [N]	
					m	*h*
He	*decided on*	*the*	*house*	*in*	*the*	*country.*

The foregoing sections were intended to illustrate the general patterns of nominal group structure in English. There are a number of problems, however, which were not touched upon.

A constant problem in nominal group structure is the flexibility of members of the word-classes which realise the elements of structure. It is this which motivates questions of 'noun acting as adjective', 'adjective acting as noun' and so on. These questions are connected with problems of derivation, and with problems of lexis —since the word, though a grammatical unit, is the closest correspondent to a lexical item. A general answer to such problems, however, is perhaps that the question, 'what class of word is *red*?' is an unreal question (or at least requires several answers): the question should really be, 'what class of word is *red* in the groups *the reds of autumn*:*the red book*?'

There are a few problems connected with initial place in nominal group structure. It was implied that *deictics* initiated nominal group structure, as in *all the other boys*. But there is another element which may precede such items:

$$\left.\begin{array}{l} almost \\ nearly \\ very\ nearly \end{array}\right\} all\ the\ boys.$$

Such items only initiate the group when there is a pre-deictic present; we do not find:

$$\left.\begin{array}{l} *nearly \\ *almost \end{array}\right\} the\ boys.$$

Since they thus enter the nominal group structure in association with another element, it seems they ought to be treated as sub-modifiers, similar to other sub-modifiers, such as those with adjectives:

	m		h
d	e		
	s-m	adj.	
the	very	old	houses

A special instance of sub-modification occurs when there is a superlative adjective in the group, and the items *much, quite,* can initiate group structure:

$$\left.\begin{array}{l} much \\ quite \\ very\ nearly \end{array}\right\} the\ best\ house.$$

A further problem is raised by certain groups containing the item 'of':

> several of the men   five of the men   both of the men
> a lot of the men   all of the men.

If we analyse such examples as:

m	h	q	h	q
a	lot	[of the men]	both	[of the men]

the results are surely counter-intuitive. That is, lexical words such as *men* will occur merely as part of a *q* to headwords such as *lot, both*. Such examples are not, of course, to be confused with groups which do have lexical items at *h* and *of* qualifiers:

m	h	q	m	h	q
the	hearts	[of men]	a	basinful	[of joy].

D

Further comparison, and particularly a study of systems at *d* (pp. 128 *ff*) will show that the items *a lot of*, *several of*, etc., operate like deictics, and it would seem reasonable to include such compound items in the class which realises pre-deictic. This will give a more satisfactory analysis of the groups above:

m			*h*
d			
d_1	d_2		
a lot of	the	men	

m			*h*
d			
d_1	d_2		
both of	the	men	

It was stated earlier that items which occur at *m* do not usually occur at *q*. Adjectives at *e* precede their noun at *h*: but there are a number of instances where the adjective follows a noun. This is sometimes for conventional reasons, sometimes for stylistic reasons and frequently to give an appositional relationship:

(a) with certain constructions historically modelled on French:
fee simple
court martial
body politic
Postmaster General

(b) when there is more than one adjective:
a leer menacing and horrible
thoughts dear and tender

(c) when the adjective is sub-modified:
a talent so great
a joy too divine
a laugh so infectious

(d) adjectives placed after the *h* in apposition:
a man, cruel beyond belief
the woman, beautiful and clever.

Proper nouns present some problems. The type *Sunny Spain* has already been touched on. It should be added that proper nouns may be plural: *the Alps*, *the Antipodes*, and that homonyms of unique names may be used with the ordinary noun contrasts and patterns: *the Joneses, a John Smith, the young Matthews*.

2.2.2 *Verbal Group*[4]

The verbal group is one of the most complex areas of English grammar. This complexity is brought about by the fact that a relatively large number of systemic choices are made here, and there is not a one-to-one correspondence between a term in a system and an element of structure realising this choice. The same element(s) of structure may be the realisation of a number of systemic choices. Thus, a verbal group such as *is coming* will be systemically described as *finite, non-modal, active, positive, present in present, imperfective*. But we cannot say which 'bits of structure' realise which terms. The elements of structure which realise even one systemic term may not be discrete. Thus, the 'tense' of the verbal group:

(He) *will have been going to be doing* (it for a month now).

will ultimately be analysed as:

present in future in past in future,

but we do not have neatly separated elements of structure realising each component of this compound tense.

It is obvious, however, that this complexity is primarily a systemic, a deep grammar complexity. Initially the verbal group structure may be described in relatively simple terms. But when consideration is given to the various systems (pp. 131 *ff.*) a more complex description which relates the various structures to the terms they realise will be necessary.

In the structure of the verbal group there is again an obligatory element; in the verbal group this is always the final element of structure. This is called the lexical element, because (apart from the very restricted list of auxiliary verbs discussed later) any verb in the language may operate here. The simplest type of verbal group will therefore be one having only a lexical element of structure. Thus:

$$\left.\begin{array}{l} comes \\ walks \\ fought \\ swindled \\ fire \end{array}\right\} \text{ structure: } l$$

There is an element of structure which may precede the lexical element. This is called the auxiliar element, and the verbs operating at this element are called auxiliary verbs. The structure of such groups will therefore be auxiliar + lexical element. Thus:

$$\left.\begin{array}{l} \textit{will come} \\ \textit{can come} \\ \textit{is coming} \\ \textit{will eat} \\ \textit{has eaten} \end{array}\right\} \text{structure: } al$$

There are only eleven members of the class of auxiliary verb, so they can easily be listed:

> *be, have, do, will/would, shall/should, can/could, may/might, must, ought, dare, need.*

Auxiliary verbs are differentiated from lexical verbs by a number of criteria, morphological and syntactic. The morphology of auxiliary verbs differs from that of lexical verbs (pp. 45–46) in that the auxiliary verbs have either more or less forms than the lexical verbs. In syntactic function there are four main criteria by which auxiliary verbs are classified:

(1) Negation: when they operate in negative verbal groups, the auxiliary verbs regularly take the enclitic form of the negator, *n't*; the lexical verbs never take the enclitic form of the negator:

$$\left.\begin{array}{l} \textit{I can't come} \\ \textit{I mustn't go} \\ \textit{Tom didn't go} \end{array}\right\} \text{but not} \left\{\begin{array}{l} \textit{*I jumpedn't it} \\ \textit{*I hopen't so} \\ \textit{*I liken't it.} \end{array}\right.$$

(2) Inversion: auxiliary verbs are obligatory in clauses which have 'inversion', i.e. clauses which have the s included within the P. Inversion is characteristic of clauses which are interrogative, and clauses which contain semi-negative adverbs in initial position:

> *Is the boy coming?*   *Rarely had they seen such things*
> *Isn't the boy coming?*   *Scarcely had the noise subsided . . .*
> *Will he come?*   *Never have I said such a thing.*

(3) Substitution: the function of the auxiliary verb 'do' is to substitute for a lexical verb; it may substitute for any lexical verb in the language. For this reason the auxiliary verb 'do' is often said to be a 'dummy' or 'lexically empty' verb:

> *I like it and so do they*
> *I scored and so did John.*

In a linked sequence of clauses in which the verbal groups contain an auxiliary verb, only the auxiliary verb need be repeated after the first clause. The auxiliary verb is thus a substitute for the whole group:

He can come and so can John

He will play on Thursday and I think Harry will too.

Given an initial lexical verb as the 'key', such a 'code' of auxiliaries may extend across sentence boundaries in dialogue.

(4) Marked Positive Element: This is closely related to criterion (2), and may be considered here. It is possible to stress the auxiliary in a verbal group and thus stress the polarity (the 'yes-ness' or 'no-ness', p. 137) or the modality (p. 132) without stressing the 'lexi-cality' of the verb at *l*; an auxiliary verb is therefore necessary for this purpose:

He *did* hit the boy

You *must* see him

He *has* been asked

I *can* come.

When a verbal group contains an auxiliar and a lexical element, the lexical verb operating at *l* will take a non-finite form, and the auxiliary verb operating at *a* may take a non-finite form (must if it is a modal verb). It is an important distinction whether a verbal group is finite or non-finite and so—although properly this is a systemic distinction and is discussed later (p. 131)—some discussion and illustration is perhaps useful at this point. The realisation of finite-ness occurs always at the initial element of structure of the verbal group: when there is only a lexical element present the lexical verb will have either a finite or non-finite form; when there is an auxiliar element present then the auxiliary verb will occur in initial position and will determine the finiteness of the group. The forms are:

Finite	Non-finite
eats/does eat	Infinitive: *to eat/eat*
ate/did eat	*to have eaten*
will, shall eat	*to be about to eat*

beginning with:

is, has, was, had	Participle: *taking*
shall/should, can/could	*taken/having taken*
may/might, must, ought	*being about to take*
dare, need	

We can sum this up by saying that there is a system of finiteness which has the terms finite and non-finite. If finite is selected then this will be realised by the occurrence at initial position in group structure of an -s, -d or base form of the verb, or a modal: if non-finite is selected then this will be realised at initial position in group structure by the occurrence of the t-inf, base-inf, -ing, -en form of the auxiliary if present, or the lexical verb if there is no auxiliary.

System	Terms	Realisation (*at initial element*)
Finiteness⟶	⌜finite————➤	-s, -d, base form; or a modal
	⌞non-finite———➤	-ing, -en, t-inf., base-inf.

There are four basic types of compound verbal group involving the occurrence of an auxiliar and a lexical element. These are given below, and are discussed here in terms of structure only, but some brief notes are made indicating the nature of the systemic features which the various structures realise, and which are discussed in more detail later.

(i) *auxiliary verb* + *-ing form of the lexical verb*
The auxiliary verb in this structure is realised by a form of the *be*, as in:

> *is coming*
> *was coming*
> *were coming.*

This structure is particularly associated with 'tense' and 'aspect'; ('continuous present', etc.) in English; in the later discussion an attempt is made to show that these are different systems, and should be treated separately in description.

(ii) *auxiliary verb* + *-en form of the lexical verb*
The auxiliary verb in this structure is realised either by (a) a form of the verb *have*, as in:

> *has bitten*
> *had bitten,*

or (b) a form of the verb *be*, as in:

> *is bitten*
> *was bitten.*

We clearly have two different sub-structures here, and—as would be expected—they realise different systemic features. The structure with *have* is like (i) in that it is associated with features of tense and aspect.

The structure with *be* occurs as a realisation of the term passive in the system of voice.

(iii) *auxiliary verb* + *the base form of the lexical verb*
The auxiliary verb in this structure is realised by a member of a subset of auxiliary verbs called modal verbs, as in:

> *can swim*
> *must go*
> *will play.*

The features which are realised by the modal verbs in English are complicated; but the various shades of meaning can be discussed in general terms of 'obligation, duty' and the like. A problem is posed by the auxiliary verbs *will* and *shall*: these verbs are usually said to be primarily concerned with tense, in particular future tense. But they certainly do not only express tense, and by their occurrence in this structure may correctly be classed as modal verbs.

(iv) *auxiliary verb* + *t-inf. form of the lexical verb*
The auxiliary verb in this structure is realised by a restricted set of modals—*ought, have, be* (the *have* and *be* in this structure are different in function from the *have* and *be* in (i) and (ii) above), as in:

> *he ought to go*
> *he has to go*
> *he is to go.*

This structure should not be confused with examples such as:

> *he wanted to go*
> *he hoped to go,*

in which, it is argued below (pp. 59 *ff*), we have two predicators in clause structure, and not a compound verbal group realising one predicator in clause structure.

We may return to the auxiliary verbs, and in particular to their subclassification which was mentioned briefly above. There are morphological and syntactic criteria by which the auxiliary verbs may be subclassified. In terms of morphology, auxiliary verbs form into five distinct classes:

(1) *Be:* this is the only verb in English which has five finite forms—*am, are, is; was were*: it also has a base-inf., a t-inf., an -ing and an -en form.

(2) *Have:* this verb has three finite forms (*have, has, had*); it also has a base-inf., a t-inf. and an -ing form; it has no -en form.

(3) *Do:* this verb has three finite forms (*do, does, did*), but no non-finite forms (though the full verb *do* has non-finite forms).

(4) *Will, shall, can, may:* these verbs have two finite forms (*will/would, shall/should, can/could, may/might*), but no non-finite forms, and no -s forms.

(5) *Must, ought, dare, need:* these verbs have only one finite form, and no non-finite forms.

If we take as a criterion the presence or absence of -s forms, these auxiliary verbs fall into two classes:

with -s form: *be, have, do* (call these non-modal)

without -s forms: *will, shall, can, must, ought, dare, need* (call these modal).

A similar classification is derived from the syntax of the auxiliaries in relation to the four basic structures discussed above. These were:

(i) aux. + -ing

(ii) aux. + -en

(iii) aux. + base

(iv) aux. + t-inf.

In operation in these structures, the verbs *be, have* occur with -ing and -en forms, i.e. structures (i) and (ii), but not with the base or t-inf. forms, i.e. structures (iii) and (iv); the verbs *will, shall, may, must, dare, need, can, ought* (*be, have*) occur with either the base or t-inf. forms, i.e. structures (iii) and (iv), but not with the -ing or -en forms, i.e. structures (i) and (ii). The verb *do* occurs with structure (iii), but its overall patterning is unlike the other modals; it is unlike *be* and *have* in occurring in structure (iii), but it is more like them than it is like the modals and it is already classed with them morphologically. So we may class the auxiliary verbs as follows:

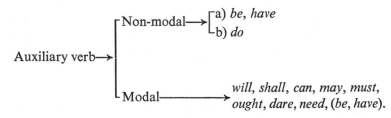

These are some problems connected with the identification of some auxiliary verbs which also have lexical verb forms. The verb *be* is exceptional both in morphology and syntax; it is already evident that there are (at least) three *be* verbs in English, as in:

(i) *The world is round*
(ii) *a He is eating*
    b He is eaten
(iii) *He is to leave immediately.*

In (i) the form *is* is the only realisation of the verbal group at P in clause structure. It must therefore realise the *l* element of the group, so must be a lexical verb. In (ii) *a* and *b* the auxiliary realises the auxiliar element of structures (i) and (ii) above, and so is an auxiliary non-modal verb concerned with the realisation of features of aspect and tense and voice. In (iii) the form *is* occurs with the pattern of structure (iv) above, and is an auxiliary modal verb concerned with modal function of 'obligation, duty'.

Dare and *need* also present some problems, and perhaps remind us that, as was said regarding word-classes in the nominal group, we cannot properly identify items in isolation, but only as they occur in syntagms. The verbs *dare* and *need* are characterised as being auxiliaries by taking the enclitic negator and by inversion:

    He daren't go   *Dare we go?*
    You needn't ask   *Need they suffer like this?*

and are further characterised as auxiliaries by having no -s forms: we do not find— *daresn't he? *needsn't he?
On the other hand, we shall find:

    He doesn't dare to go   *Do they dare us?*
    You don't need to ask   *Do they need to ask?*

where the presence of *do* in the negative and inverted structures shows that *do* is the auxiliary verb and *dare* and *need* are lexical verbs. It is also evident that in:

    He dares to call me a coward   *You dare to say that*
    He needs to be examined   *They need to have their tea*

they are lexical verbs, because they have distinct -s forms, and because they occur in structure (iv), not structure (iii).

It is obvious from what has been said that there is a negative (*n*) element in verbal group structure in addition to *a* and *l*. This, indeed, is one element of structure in the verbal group which does stand in a one-to-one relation with the choice of a term in a system: the choice of negative (rather than positive) in the system of polarity is always realised by the presence of the negator (*not, n't*) in the verbal group. The list of primary elements of structure of the verbal group is therefore:

$$\overrightarrow{(a), (n),}\ l$$

where, as before, brackets indicate optional elements of structure, the arrow indicates obligatory sequence, and the commas indicate this is a list of elements of structure, not a structure. Thus:

structure:	*l*	*al*	*anl*
	comes	*will come*	*will not come*
	taken	*will take*	*won't take*
	votes	*did vote*	*didn't vote.*

Longer verbal groups can be described as combinations of the four basic types. This means that when two or more auxiliary verbs occur in the verbal group they will combine with each other and finally with the lexical verb in sequences of the four types. We can primarily give the structure of such groups, and then describe the combinations involved in terms of the four basic types. Thus:

will be taking   structure: *aal*; (iii), (i).

And so

will have taken   structure: *aal*; (iii), (ii)$^{a \cdot}$
will be taken   structure: *aal*; (iii), (ii)$^{b \cdot}$
will have been taken   structure: *aaal*; (iii), (ii)$^{a \cdot}$, (ii)$^{b \cdot}$
will have been being taken   structure: *aaaal*; (iii), (ii)$^{a \cdot}$, (i), (ii)$^{b \cdot}$
ought to have been taken   structure: *aaal*; (iv), (ii)$^{a \cdot}$, (ii)$^{b \cdot}$

There is one further point of verbal group structure to be considered. If the clause, *he decided on the ship* means 'he made up his mind while he was on the ship' then the structure is SPA:

S	P	A
he	*decided*	*on the ship*

but if it means 'he chose the ship' then the structure is SPC and the P is realised by a phrasal verb:

S	P	C
he	*decided on*	*the ship.*

There are many instances in English where verb + particle (preposition or adverb) operates as a single unit. We can often replace the verb + particle with a simple verb, as in:

He put down the rebellion: *He suppressed the rebellion*
She looked after her mother: *She tended her mother.*

Also, in passive constructions the particle remains with the verb:

The ship was decided on
Her mother was looked after
He was looked up to by his fellows.

It is also the case that which particles go with which verbs (and with which meaning) is restricted: *look up to* but not *look down to* (but—*look down on*); *take to* but not *take from*.

Such criteria are usually cited to show that verb + particle form a single unit in such structures, and realise the element P (C) in clause structure; and are therefore different from verb + adverb realising the elements P (A) in clause structure.

The concept of the phrasal verb, as this structure is usually called, is well established in grammatical description, and is a valid concept. But it must be said that the identification of phrasal verbs in particular structures often relies heavily on semantic criteria, and there is often room for disagreement; the line between phrasal verb + nominal group (PC) and verb + adverb or preposition (+ nominal group) is very difficult to draw.

Nevertheless, there are many examples where the difference is clear, and many long-established phrasal verbs can be easily recognised, as in:

S	P	A	S	P	C
We	went	to the place:	We	took to	the place.

2.2.3 *Adverbial Group*

There are two distinct types of adverbial group in English, but they are initially classed together because they both realise the element A(djunct) in clause structure. They may be secondarily classified (on morphological grounds) as 'adverb-headed' adverbial group, and 'preposition-headed' adverbial group.

As the name suggests, the first type has the traditional 'adverb' operating at an element of its structure. This is the obligatory element of structure in the first type of adverbial group; groups with only this element are common, particularly as realisations of 'grammatical' adjuncts (p. 63): *if, that, because, though* and the like. Other typical realisations of this element are:

beautifully	*swiftly*	*fast*	*well*
nicely	*now*	*quickly*	*adverbially*
comfortably	*then*	*there*	*soon.*

This element of structure is called the *apex*,[5] and the simplest structure of this type of group is therefore one with only an *a* element, as in:

I run *fast*   I'll do it *now*   she sings *beautifully*.

There is an element of structure which may precede the *a* element; this is called the temperer (*t*), and at this element operate submodifiers such as *very, more, as, right, nearly, just, exactly, over.* Thus:

$$\left.\begin{array}{l}\textit{very nicely} \\ \textit{right there} \\ \textit{over here} \\ \textit{just before}\end{array}\right\} \text{structure: } ta$$

There is also an element of structure which may follow the *a* element; this is called the limiter, and a restricted range of realisations occur here, some of which correlate with items occurring at *t*. A unique item, *enough*, occurs at *l* when there is no *t* element, as in:

$$\left.\begin{array}{l}\textit{nicely enough} \\ \textit{quickly enough}\end{array}\right\} \text{structure: } al$$

Another single word item, *indeed*, correlates very often with *very* at *t*, as in:

$$\left.\begin{array}{l}\textit{very quickly indeed} \\ \textit{very nicely indeed} \\ \textit{very fast indeed}\end{array}\right\} \text{structure: } tal$$

When certain items occur at *t*, typically *more* and *as*, the *l* element is realised by *than/as* + a nominal group or a clause, as in:

$$\left.\begin{array}{l}\text{(He ran) } \textit{more quickly than last time} \\ \text{(He runs) } \textit{more quickly than Tom can run} \\ \text{(He ran) } \textit{as fast as a hare} \\ \text{(He ran) } \textit{as fast as his legs would carry him.}\end{array}\right\} \text{structure: } tal$$

The list of elements for this type of adverbial group is therefore:

$$\overrightarrow{(t), a, (l).}$$

The second ('preposition-headed') type of adverbial group has two elements of structure, both of which must be present. These are called the prepend, at which operates the word-class preposition, and completive, at which operates a rankshifted nominal group. The list of elements of structure for this type of group is therefore:

$$\overrightarrow{pc.}$$

The similarity of symbols to the *pc* of clause structure is intended to reflect the similarity of the 'transitivity' of prepositions and verbs; this type of group is often described as a 'minor predication' in the clause. Thus:

$$\left.\begin{array}{l}\textit{up the hill} \\ \textit{in the road} \\ \textit{on the roof} \\ \textit{under the counter}\end{array}\right\} \text{structure: } pc$$

A number of items occur which seem best treated as compound

prepositions operating at *p* in an adverbial group. Indeed, the difference between some 'multi-word' prepend realisations and single word prepend realisations is often no more than spelling convention. Compounds are frequent with the item *of* (recalling some problems of nominal group structure). Thus:

p	*c*	*p*	*c*	*p*	*c*
out of	*the river*	*in spite of*	*the wind*	*apart from*	*him*

p	*c*	*p*	*c*	*p*	*c*
because of	*the snow*	*in front of*	*the house*	*due to*	*the rain.*

There are two modifications to be made to this general picture. First, it was stated that the element *c* was always realised by a rankshifted nominal group, but there are some structures which seem best described as *pc* adverbial groups in which *c* is realised by an adverb. Thus:

$$\left.\begin{array}{l} until\ recently \\ until\ then \\ from\ now \\ before\ now \end{array}\right\} \text{structure: } pc$$

Second, there are a number of items which can operate before the *p* element of a *pc* adverbial group. We may denote this element (quite arbitrarily) as *o*. A restricted, but fairly wide, range of items realise this element. Items such as *very, nearly, quite* typically precede the prepositions *near, like,* as in:

$$\left.\begin{array}{l} very\ near\ the\ house \\ very\ like\ the\ last\ one \end{array}\right\} \text{structure: } opc$$

Other items, which occur with numerous prepositions, are:

> *just, right, straight, almost, half, right to, just for,*

as in:

$$\left.\begin{array}{l} just\ under\ the\ surface \\ straight\ from\ town \\ almost\ over\ the\ top \\ right\ from\ under\ him \end{array}\right\} \text{structure: } opc$$

2.3   Group and Clause

As we move up the rankscale, while no unit is in any sense more important than any other, the potentiality of structural complexity is increased. This is structurally obvious in three ways:

(i) Sequence is less determined. Elements of structure are not effectively defined by position alone. At the lower ranks we had elements of structure such as *pbf* where *p* and *f* were defined by position, as occurring before and after the *b* element, so we could generalise and symbolise as $\overrightarrow{pbf}$. Similarly, in group structure we had $\overrightarrow{mhq}$, $\overrightarrow{tal}$, $\overrightarrow{pc}$. In clause structure we will have four elements of structure—SPCA— but actual occurring structures will exhibit various combinations and sequences of these—SAP, PCA, ASPC and so on.

(ii) Elements occur recursively, or in depth. This was already evident in word and group structure:

$$f^1 \quad f^2$$
$$kind + li + ness$$
$$e^2 \quad e^1$$
lush green grass
$$n^3 \quad n^2 \quad n^1$$
subscriber trunk dialling system.

But at the ranks of clause and sentence this becomes more marked and complex.

(iii) The occurrence of inclusion or discontinuity. That is, one unit occurring within the lineal representation of, but not rankshifted into the structure of, another unit; or (looking at it the other way) a unit being discontinuous in that its elements of structure are in-terrupted by another unit. Thus, s included in P in clause structure (discontinuous P):

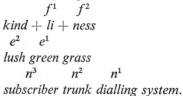

P S P
Is John coming?

Clause included within the structure of another clause (discontinuous element of sentence structure):

John,//if you give him a ring,//will come over.

As mentioned already, there are four elements of clause structure initially, to which are given the names s(ubject), P(redicator), c(omplement), A(djunct). There is no obligatory element of structure in the English clause. It is often said that P is obligatory (and some-times s) but many clauses occur without a P, and many clauses occur without an s (and it is not necessary to claim that they must be 'understood'). The elements of structure of the clause must therefore all be listed with brackets if the most generalised statement is to be given. It is, however, true that the distinction between clauses containing a P and clauses not containing a P is a very important one. Clauses containing a P are called major, and clauses not containing a P are called minor. Major clauses have thus a list of elements of structure:

(S), P, (C), (A)

The problem of identifying these elements of structure is some-what different from that at lower ranks, partly because of the variability of sequence. It is usually said that the main criterion for identification of s (if we ignore semantic definitions such as 'the thing being talked about') is concord with P, as in *the bird sings* but *the birds sing*. This means that a nominal group which can commute with a gender bearing pronoun (*he, she, it*), or one of these pronouns at *h*, requires the -s form of the verb at P when the tense is 'non-past'. In past tense verbal forms this concord is not marked. So that, for identifying s, concord means that a gender bearing nominal group requires the -s form of the verb where that form is possible. Thus, in the clause, *that man makes the suits* there are two nominal groups; *that man* can commute with *he*—a gender bearing pronoun, but *the suits* can only be replaced by the genderless *they/them* (we cannot say *the suits* can be replaced only by *them*, the complement form of *they*, until we have in fact decided that *the suits* is the complement). In this clause, therefore, it is *that man* which correlates with the -s form of the verb, and since the -s form does occur in the clause then *that man* is identified as s. Similarly, in the clause *those men make the suit* it is *the suit* which can be replaced by a gender bearing pronoun (*it*), and would require the -s form of the verb if it were s; since the -s form of the verb does not occur, then it must be *those men* which is s. But the clauses in which the s can be identified in this way are restricted; in any of the following it is not possible:

that man makes the suit
those men make the suits
that man made the suit
that man made the suits
those men made the suit
those men made the suits.

Thus concord, though important in English, will only identify s in a small number of possible structures. We normally, in fact, identify by sequence alone. We take the s to be that nominal group which immediately precedes the verbal group; so in either of the clauses *he saw the film*

the film he saw (but not the play)

he is identified as s.

The element P is identified by concord and sequence. We have already morphologically identified P as one or more verbal group(s), i.e. as having a different pattern from the nominal group. The clause *the boy will bite the dog* contains two examples of the nominal group pattern and one example of the verbal group pattern. When we consider these groups syntactically we find that the sequence nominal–verbal–nominal is very common, and that certain members of the verbal group are realised by the -s form of the verb when preceded by certain members of the nominal group; and further, the sequence nominal–verbal often occurs alone, and is invariable, though the second nominal, when present, may alter position, as in the clauses

he saw the film

the film he saw (but not the play).

Concord relations between what we have called s and the verbal group, which we can now say is at P, are mutually defining, as is sequence.

The element c is like s in that it is realised by one or more nominal group(s). Identification of c is already made, since we can say it is that nominal group which is not the s of the clause.

Adverbial groups realise the element A in clause structure. In theory any number of adjuncts may occur in a clause, but there are some restrictions which will be considered later.

This four-element picture of English clause structure is, however, complicated by the fact that there are situations where we can morphologically identify a nominal group operating in the clause, but we cannot identify it as s or c of the clause syntactically. In the clauses

they want the boys to do it

if wet, (the show will be cancelled)

Bill, shoot/shoot, Bill

the items *the boys, wet, Bill* can be identified as nominal groups but not as s or c. Such nominal groups are said to realise a z element of clause structure. The reason for inability to identify the groups as operating at s or c is not the same in each case; we have, in fact, three different types of z element:

(i) In the first of these clauses the nominal group *the boys* is the c of *want* and the s of *to do*. This is called a z *positive* element (z^{pos}), since it is positively identified as a conflation of s and c. (See further, pp. 59 *ff*.)

(ii) In the second clause, *if wet*, the nominal group cannot be identified as s or c because identification of these elements depends on concord and sequence relationships with P, and this is a minor clause. In distinction from the previous type, this is called a z *negative* (z^{neg}).

(iii) The third clause is not a minor clause, nor is the nominal group, *Bill*, a conflation of s and c. Though it may immediately precede s, it is marked off from the rest of the clause by a comma (an intonation break in the spoken language), and is variable in position—it follows the P in the second form of the clause. This element is called a z *vocative* (z^{voc}). (See further, pp. 94–95.)

The general picture of English clauses (and clause is perhaps one of the areas to teach early, and certainly the best area for breaking into the analysis of texts) is that the structure of the clause is composed of some configuration of these five elements:

Predicator (realised by one or more than one verbal group)
subject ⎤
Complement ⎬ (realised by one or more than one nominal group)
z element ⎦
Adjunct (realised by one or more than one adverbial group)

The relations holding between these elements of clause structure are in some ways different from those holding between elements of structure of other units. There is perhaps no automatic procedure for recognising a clause in English; a working guide is that any structure whose elements stand in any of the possible SPCAZ relations is a clause. This means that there are no restrictions such as 'a clause must contain a finite verb', 'a clause must contain a subject'. In each of the following sentences there are two clauses:

Having read the book, I won't go to the film

For John to take advantage of the offer, all his friends contributed.

Each of the first clauses exhibits PC relations, and the first clause of the second sentence exhibits SP relation also; they can also commute with clauses which do contain finite verbal groups:

Now that I have read the book, I won't go to the film

So that John could take advantage of the offer, all his friends contributed.

E

There is, however, a crucial difference between the clauses in each of the sentences. The second clause in each can occur alone, as the realisation of a sentence; the first clause in each cannot. Such clauses are called independent and dependent clauses respectively. The main criteria for the identification of independent and dependent clauses are:

Independent	*Dependent*
(i) absence of 'binding' adjunct	presence of 'binding' adjunct: *who, which, what, when, where, how, that, if, because, although, provided that, in case, in case that,* etc.
(ii) presence of finite verbal group at P obligatory	presence of non-finite verbal group at P: *a*) infinitive: *To take part in the game,* he came home. John was the one, *the man to carry it.* *b*) participle: *The windows being open,* the room was cool. *Their king captured,* the enemy surrendered.

Dependent clauses may be secondarily classified according to what is called the 'vector of dependence' into additioning, conditioning and reported clauses.

The dependent additioning clause corresponds to the non-defining relative clause of traditional grammar. Such a clause cannot occur before the independent clause to which it is bound, though it can occur within ('be included in') it, or can follow it. Thus:

My young brother, *who is very tall,* plays the game well

I am shorter than my brother, *who plays the game well.*

Such clauses have a relative binding adjunct at initial place in structure—*who, which, when, where, how; in whom/which, by whom/which,* etc. It should be noted that the item *that* does not introduce such clauses, though it does introduce rankshifted (restricted) clauses.

The dependent conditioning clause corresponds approximately

to the adverbial clause of traditional grammar. It can occur before, within or after the independent clause to which it is bound. Thus:

If you bring them, John will help you

John will help you, *if you bring them*

John, *if you bring them,* will help you.

Such clauses have either a non-finite verbal group at P, as in

John being in no mood to delay, the trip was started early

The empire conquered by the barbarians, the last of the Romans took his own life

or have a binding adjunct such as *after, as, as if, as soon as, because, if, though,* etc.

The dependent reported clause corresponds approximately to the traditional noun clause of indirect speech. Such a clause follows the independent clause to which it is bound, as in

He said *that it was true*

He declared *it was a fact.*

Such a clause may have an initial binding adjunct such as *that, whether, if*; but it may occur without such an adjunct. Reported clauses follow 'reporting' clauses which typically have a 'reporting' verb at P: *expect, feel, find out, hear, imagine, say, tell, inform, claim, shout,* etc.

2.3.1 *Complements in Clause Structure*

The element C in clause structure is identified as that nominal group (or those groups) which is (are) not in S relation to P. Not all English clauses contain a C in their structure; some clauses contain one C, and some contain two C's. Clauses which do contain a C element are called transitive, and clauses may be transitive single (containing one C) or transitive double (containing two C's); clauses which do not contain a C element are called intransitive.

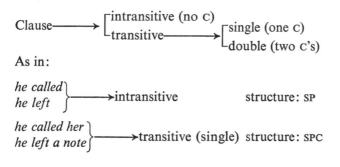

Clause⟶ [intransitive (no C) / transitive ⟶ [single (one C) / double (two C's)]

As in:

he called / *he left* ⟶ intransitive   structure: SP

he called her / *he left a note* ⟶ transitive (single) structure: SPC

> *he called her a beauty*⎫
> *he called her a cab* ⎬──────→transitive (double) structure: SPCC

If, however, we consider the clauses
  (i) *Bill bought a new car* or *he called her a cab*
  (ii) *Bill felt fine* or *he called her a beauty*
we recognise intuitively that although both (i) and (ii) contain complements, there are different types of c involved. The distinction between the c's is in part a reflection of the difference between noun-headed nominal groups and adjective-headed nominal groups. Those nominal groups which have an adjective operating at *h* may realise the element c in clause structure, but not the element s. Nominal groups which have a noun operating at *h* may realise either c or s in clause structure. Adjective-headed nominal groups cannot normally operate at *c* in a *pc* type adverbial group, but noun-headed groups can. That is, we can have *in the building* but not **in happy*. Noun-headed groups can commute with pronimals, as:
  the man──────→*he/him*
  the trees──────→*they/them*
but not adjective-headed groups,
  very happy──────→**—*.

The different types of complement are called extensive (noun-headed) and intensive (adjective-headed). But, though it is true that adjective-headed complements are always intensive, it is not true that all intensive complements are adjective-headed groups; the clause *Bill felt fit* could be rendered *Bill felt a fit man* where *a fit man* is an intensive complement, but is a noun-headed nominal group. So the relation is only one way: given an adjective-headed group at c we can say the c is intensive; but given an intensive complement, we cannot say it will be realised by an adjective-headed group.

The main point to be made is that clauses containing an extensive complement will have a passive transform; that is, any grammatical clause which has an extensive complement will have a related clause which has the P in the passive voice and whose s is the extensive complement of the original.
  Bill bought a new car──────→*A new car was bought by Bill.*
This is not so with clauses containing only an intensive complement.
          but not
  Bill felt fine──────→**Fine was felt by Bill.*
Contextually, intensive means having the same referent as some

previous element of clause structure (*fine* refers to *Bill*); extensive means not having the same referent as something previously mentioned. Superscript can be used to denote the different types: extensive complement—c^E, intensive complement—c^I.

Clauses which contain double c's will have different possibilities of transform: if both c's are extensive there will be two possible transforms. Thus:

He gave her a shilling   structure: SPC^Ec^E
She was given a shilling (by him)   structure: $SPC^E(A)$
A shilling was given her (by him)   structure: $SPC^E(A)$

If one of the c's is intensive there will only be one possible transform. Thus:

He called her a beauty   structure: SPC^Ec^I
She was called a beauty (by him)   structure: $SPC^I(A)$
not *A beauty was called her (by him)*.

A further point which may be observed from the above examples is that an intensive complement may be intensive to the s (necessarily so if there is only one c in the clause), or to another c (if there are two c's in the clause). In the clause:

He called her a beauty   structure: SPC^Ec^I

the second complement is intensive to the first; but in the clause:

He made her a good husband   structure: SPC^Ec^I

the second complement is intensive to the subject. So, for a full marking we ought to write:

He called her a beauty   structure: $SPC^Ec^{I(C)}$
He made her a good husband   structure: $SPC^Ec^{I(S)}$.

Certain verbs will operate more readily with the more complex types of structure, e.g. *buy, call, consider, make, get, leave, like*. The possible variations, using *make* are:

She made a good cake   structure: SPC^E
She made a good wife   structure: SPC^I
She made him a good cake   structure: SPC^Ec^E
She made him a good husband   structure: $SPC^Ec^{I(C)}$
She made him a good wife   structure: $SPC^Ec^{I(S)}$

2.3.2 *Predicators in Clause Structure*[6]

In discussing verbal group structure (p. 45) it was noted that sequences such as *started to bite, wanted to bite* did not fit the auxiliary + lexical pattern under consideration there. The first items are clearly not auxiliary verbs; they do not take the enclitic negator;

we do not find *started'nt to bite, *wanted'nt to bite. Nor do such structures occur in interrogative clauses; they require an auxiliary verb:

> *Will he start to do it?*
> *Does he want to bite?*

It is evident that we have two lexical elements in these structures, and since only one lexical element occurs in each verbal group we must have two verbal groups; this in turn means that we must have two predicators in the clause structure. Predicators operating in this way are called phased predicators. Thus:

> *He started to bite*   structure: SPP
> *He wanted to eat*   structure: SPP
> *He hoped to win the trophy*   structure: SPPC
> *He refused to sign the paper*   structure: SPPC

The last two examples show the occurrence of a complement after the second predicator in the phase sequence. Such phased structures also occur with a nominal group intervening between the phased predicators, with or without a complement after the second predicator. Thus:

> *He wanted Tom to do it*
> *He asked the skipper to turn the ship*
> *He begged the other to find the jewel*
> *He told the boys to go.*

In these clauses the nominal groups *Tom, the skipper, the other, the boys,* are complements of the first predicator and s of the second predicator. This is frequently illustrated in a transformational way; given the pairs of sentences:

> (i) *He asked John.*   *John does it.*
> (ii) *He told his elder brother.*   *His elder brother sold books.*
> (iii) *He begged her.*   *She returned the book.*

The complement of the first member of each pair can be conflated with the subject of the second member of each pair, and the second predicator given a non-finite form, to produce the grammatical sentences:

> (i) *He asked John to do it*
> (ii) *He told his elder brother to sell books*
> (iii) *He begged her to return the book.*

Nominal groups which conflate c and s in this way are called z elements of clause structure (p. 55), more precisely z^{pos} elements. The analysis of these clauses is therefore:

(i) *He asked John to do it*   structure: SPZPC
(ii) *He told his elder brother to sell books*   structure: SPZPC
(iii) *He begged her to return the book*   structure: SPZPC

When the intervening nominal group is the realisation of an intensive complement, however, the position is different. The clauses

He was eager to swim
He seemed content to remain
He became anxious to find her

have phased predicators and intervening nominal groups. The nominal groups are realisations of intensive complements, and are in no sense the subject of the second predicators. Since intensive complements cannot operate at s in non-phased constructions this is not surprising. They are like the first type of phase structure in that they involve only one s, (we might say one 'actor' who both 'wants' and 'eats' in *I want to eat*, and one 'actor' who 'is eager' and 'goes' in *I am eager to go*). The intensive complement, therefore, remains an intensive complement, and the analysis is:

He was eager to swim   structure: SPC^IP

Perhaps the obvious question is whether there are clauses with two 'actors' which contain intensive complements, as there are for one 'actor' clauses. The clauses

I am eager for John to do it
I was anxious for Mary to come

would seem to fill this slot. In English we do not have two nominal groups juxtaposed to introduce a second 'actor–action' sequence in a phased construction, i.e. we do not find

*I am eager John to do it
*I am anxious Mary to come

We must insert the preposition *for* before the nominal group which is s of the second predicator in the phased sequence. But such clauses are the fourth type of phase structure, and it seems best to analyse the '*for* + nominal group' (following a c^I in a phased sequence) as the realisation of a z element of clause structure. This gives us four types of phased structures, two with one 'actor', and two with two 'actors'. Thus:

I hope to attend   structure: SPP
I am keen to attend   structure: SPC^IP
I asked John to attend   structure: SPZP
I am keen for John to attend   structure: SPC^IZP

Phased structures involve what are often called 'linking' or 'catenative' verbs, and the structures are recursive. The analysis of clauses containing more than two predicators follows naturally from the analysis of two predicator clauses. Thus:

2 p's
{ *I asked Bill to come early*   structure: SPZPA
{ *I'd like to see you for a moment*   structure: SPPCA

3 p's
⎧ *I wanted John to invite Mary to come*   structure: SPZPZP
⎨ *I began to feel reluctant to play*   structure: SPPC^{I}P
⎩ *I was eager for John to get Tom to play*   structure: SPC^{I}ZPZP

4 p's   *I told John to ask Mary to tell her brother to come*
structure SPZPZPZP

We have thus far only considered the t-inf. as the non-initial component of a phased sequence. The -ing form of the verb also occurs regularly, and—more rarely—the base form. Thus:

I detested asking him   structure: SPPC

I remember John doing it   structure: SPZPC

I kept them working   structure: SPZP

I kept working them   structure: SPPC

The shock made her faint   structure: SPZP

I saw them swim four lengths   structure: SPZPC

Phased predicators which are non-initial are always one of these non-finite forms, t-inf., base, -ing. Which form occurs will depend on the initiating verb, and verbs can be classified according to the non-finite form they take: some verbs will occur only with the t-inf. form, e.g. *seem, offer, expect*; some verbs will occur only with the -ing form, e.g. *relish, enjoy, deny*; some will occur with both these forms, e.g. *stand, feel, start*, and there may be a difference in meaning in the two structures, as in:

He stood watching the race: He stood to win a packet

A few verbs will occur with a succeeding base form, e.g. *make, feel, help*.

Since dependent clauses can occur with non-finite predicators (p. 56) it is important to distinguish between sentences which consist of two clauses (an independent and a dependent clause) and a sentence consisting of a single clause with phased predicators. The sentences

I refused, to let him know my stand in the matter

John continued, to give them the chance

I agreed, to avoid a clash in the office

have two clauses. But the sentences

I refused to let him know my stand in the matter
John continued to give them the chance
I agreed to avoid a clash in the office

have one clause with phased predicators.

The difference between the two-clause and one-clause sentence is that sequence is variable in the former but not in the latter; we can have

To let him know my stand in the matter, I refused
To give them the chance, John continued

but not

*To do it he asked them
*To give them the chance he continued;

the non-finite part of a phased structure must follow the finite part, and there is no possibility of an intonation break in the spoken language or comma in the written language. Sentences with two clauses regularly have an intonation break or comma between the clauses. It is also the case that if a binding adverbial group can be inserted without any change in meaning then we must have two clauses and not a phased structure. Thus:

He began, asking for their help: After asking for their help, he began

with which compare

He began asking for their help.

2.3.3 Adjuncts in Clause Structure

The number and position of subject, predicator, complement, in clause structure are fairly restricted (allowing for phase); but there is no theoretical limit to the number of adjuncts which can occur in clause structure, and there is more variability of position. The positions are, however, restricted by the class of adjunct.

(i) 'Grammatical' or 'binding' adjuncts are those adjuncts which bind dependent clauses to independent clauses, and these occur at initial position; their position is fixed. We can call this position 1:

A S P C
1

(ii) Position 2 for adjuncts is between s and p; at this position operate the 'semi-negative' adverbs particularly. These adjuncts are perhaps halfway between 'grammatical' and lexical adjuncts. Typical realisations are: *never, usually, scarcely, seldom, hardly, nearly, even, just, merely, only, quite, always.* Thus:

> *He never managed to do it*
> *I usually go to the Christmas service*
> *I seldom find much of interest in his books.*

The structure of the verbal group at P in these clauses is *l*; if the verbal group at P has the structure *al* then the Adjunct occurs between these elements. Thus:

> *He did manage to do it*
> *I don't usually go to the Christmas service*
> *I would seldom find much of interest in his books.*

There is no difference in position of the adjunct involved here, it depends entirely on the structure of the verbal group. We may call this position 2:

> S A P C
> 2

(iii) Other adjuncts, and in this case the adjuncts are 'lexical', occur in clause final position. Adjuncts which are realised by a *pc* type adverbial group occur here, and many adverbial groups in -ly. Thus:

> *He crashed the car into the wall*
> *He crashed the car violently.*

We can call this position 3:

> A P C A
> 3

Further problems concerning adjuncts are in identifying different types of adjuncts, usually into adjuncts of time, place, manner, and deciding which sequence of these occurs if more than one is present in clause structure. That is, if the two adjuncts *to the shop* (place) and *immediately* (time) are to occur in position 3 in the clause beginning *He sent her* . . . will the sequence be time, place or vice versa? The preferred sequence in English seems to be place, time, manner. That is,

> *He sent her to the shop immediately* rather than *He sent her immediately to the shop*
> *He went to the block with a smile* rather than *He went with a smile to the block.*

But the sequences are preferred and by no means fixed; different varieties of English seem to follow different principles; and it is certainly the case that the mobility of adjuncts is utilised 'stylistic-ally', i.e.—the occurrence of adjuncts in 'marked' or 'thematic' positions (see pp. 97 *ff.*). A large and objective survey is required to determine the main lines.

2.4 *Clause and Sentence*

There are well over two hundred definitions of the unit sentence. These fall into various groups or types of definition; each group usually adds to, or contradicts, the others. Most grammarians seem to have found it necessary to correct and improve part or all of the previous definitions of sentence, before each produced *the* definition (which it never was, of course). Two things are immediately obvious from this: i) grammarians are unanimous in recognising the *sentence*, but ii) definition of this unit is very difficult.

Many attempts at definition were found to be unsatisfactory or inadequate because they relied solely on meaning, and attempted to delimit the sentence as being 'a complete thought/meaning/idea', or even 'the number of ideas that can be grasped in their relation in one act of attention'. But the necessary pre-definition of 'thought/idea' and so on (whether or not 'complete') makes such definitions untenable and unworkable.

A second major approach attempts to delimit the sentence by reference to its constituent elements. In this type of definition we are told that the 'secret' of the sentence is to 'name some object or place or person or thing' and then to 'say something about that object or place or person or thing'. Such definitions usually say that we need a subject and a predicator to make a sentence. This means that most commands, exclamations and requests would not be con-sidered sentences. In such instances, of course, the s is often said to be 'understood'. But how much (or little) can be 'understood'? If we are allowed to 'supply' elements then any expression can be made to conform to the definition. And it should be noted that such definitions usually state not only that a s must be present, but that the s is 'the thing being talked about'. Even in the simplest of sentences, say *John shot Jim* are we talking about *John* or *Jim* (after all, it may be his last chance to be talked about), or *shooting*? Or, as seems more reasonable, about *John shooting Jim*?

It is not a question of whether such definitions are 'true' or 'false'; only that they do not provide reliable criteria for grammatical description. There are obvious correlations between many of the definitions and occurring English sentence types. There is good reason for the recurring insistence on completeness; but it is not necessarily a 'thought/idea' which is complete. There is also good reason for trying to find a universal semantic component in sentences; sentence is typically the unit with which English works in contexts of situation: each language will have such a unit and perhaps this may be called sentence; but the grammatical description of sentence will be re-defined for each language.

There was, in fact, confusion of levels in many definitions: the sentence can be described contextually (in terms of meaning), grammatically (in terms of form), phonologically (in terms of intonation) or orthographically (in terms of punctuation). But these are different descriptions, and only after describing at these separate levels should we describe their interrelations.

The orthographic definition is frequently used; a sentence is defined as a stretch of language which begins with a capital letter and ends with a full stop, question mark or exclamation mark. This is, in fact, a valid working identification of a sentence, and even many of those who advocate a theoretical definition of sentence work with this definition in practice. In most varieties of present-day English orthographic sentences and grammatical sentences do tend to coincide. But this cannot be applied absolutely; in older texts we may have absence of punctuation or an alien system of punctuation, and numerous present-day writers have idiosyncratic systems of punctuation.

There are also certain correlations in the spoken language with grammatical sentences, certain stress patterns, intonation contours and breaks. Again this is a fair working guide, but the correlations are not always realised in practice, and it is very often impossible to tell what grammatical division is indicated by intonation patterns.

The completeness of the sentence has been increasingly recognised as a formal completeness. Most linguists have tended to follow Bloomfield's definition:

'. . . an independent linguistic form [unit] not included by virtue of any grammatical construction in any longer linguistic form [unit].'

This definition does not seem inadequate, and for the present model of grammar may perhaps be paraphrased 'A sentence is that unit which does not operate in the structure of any higher (grammatical) unit.' The whole difficulty of defining the sentence stems from the fact that it is the highest unit on the rankscale. Other units are identified and defined by their operation at elements of structure in the unit next above; thus, group is that unit which operates in clause structure, morpheme is that unit which operates in word structure, and so on. But, in the case of sentence, there is no higher grammatical unit, so that sentence cannot be defined syntactically.

It should be noted that sentences may, of course, be part of some larger linguistic context. The completeness or independence of the sentence is relative to this, because sentences which contain pronominals or anaphoric determiners will necessarily be related to the antecedents of these pronominals or anaphoric determiners. Thus:

He became headmaster of Rugby
The boys turned the corner, ran down the lane and vanished
That house has stood up well to the gale

are sentences in which the referents of *He*, *the* (*boys*), *the* (*corner*), *the* (*lane*); *that* (*house*) must be given by cotext or context if the sentences are to be understood correctly. But since there is no grammatical unit above the sentence, this inter-sentence connection cannot be completely accounted for grammatically. It is, of course, a linguistic matter, and will be of importance for stylistic studies: indeed, one linguist has defined stylistics as 'grammar above the sentence'.

We cannot, therefore, classify sentences according to their operation in the structure of the unit next above; the classification must be effected in a different way from the classification of other units. The most obvious way is by morphology; we have taken as a principle that morphology is subsidiary to syntax in grammatical classification, but in the case of sentence there is no syntax. It seems important to stress that the morphology of the sentence is not the morphology of the clause; numerous grammars talk of the subject (etc.) of the sentence, and exemplify with simple (i.e. one-clause) sentences. But compound sentences may contain a number of clauses, and therefore a number of subjects (etc.), no one of which can be called the subject of the sentence. s, P, C, A are elements of clause structure: it is complete clauses which operate at elements of sentence structure.

Classification in terms of morphology will yield a primary division into simple sentences (containing one clause) and compound sentences (containing more than one clause). Compound sentences may contain a succession of independent clauses, or may contain an independent and a dependent clause, or may contain a number of independent and a number of dependent clauses. We can name these compound, complex and compound–complex respectively. Thus:

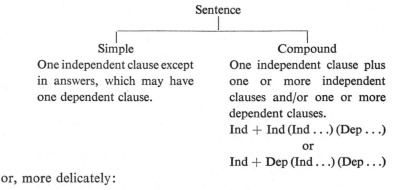

or, more delicately:

Simple   (one constituent clause)
                          Compound (more than one Ind clause)
Non-simple→ Complex (one Ind and one Dep clause or more)
                          Compound–Complex (more than one Ind and Dep)

It is also usual to classify sentences contextually into statement, question and command. There are certain correlations between these contextual classes and punctuation marks:

. statement
? question
! command/exclamation

and with certain intonation contours. They also correlate to a considerable extent with types of response, in that statement is often accompanied by 'continuation signals' (a-huh, go-on, ye-es), command is often followed by action response ('Shut the door') and question by oral response or action response; it is also true that in the case of the simple sentence there are correlations with clause classes to a large extent:

statement   declarative
question   interrogative
command   imperative.

But the correlations are not one-to-one; there are sentences realised by a declarative clause which may be contextually classified as commands, and so on; in particular minor (and therefore moodless) clauses can usually be assigned to a contextual class of sentence (see pp. 75–76 *ff.*).

Since the simple sentence is by definition coterminous with the one constituent clause there is little more to say about its structure.

Compound sentences consist of more than one clause, and this raises an immediate question of contextual class: which clause determines the contextual class of the *sentences*. In the sentences:

> *I came and I saw and I conquered*
> *Do this or do that*
> *Will you stay here or will you go to Canada?*

we find, in fact, that there are no problems. The linker *and* conjoins like items, and therefore the contextual class of any of the clauses (considered as a simple sentence) will be the contextual class of the sentence. Thus:

> *I came and I saw and I conquered*   statement
> *Do this or do that*   command
> *Will you stay here or will you go away?*   question.

In the sentences:

> *Tell him to come home when the game's over*
> *John cut the rope after Bill had shouted*
> *Keeping to the old route, Bill got home safely*

both independent and dependent clauses are involved. It is only the independent clauses which affect the contextual class of sentence. If we alter the first sentence to *Will you tell him to come home when the game's over?* the contextual class changes from command to question. If we alter the dependent clause this does not change the contextual class of sentence:

> *Tell him to come home when the game's over*   command
> *Tell him to come home if he's finished*   command.

It can be seen at this point that there are two elements of sentence structure, one of which is obligatory. The obligatory element is distinguished by two criteria: i) it can stand alone as a simple sentence; ii) it decides the contextual class of the sentence.

The obligatory element of structure is called alpha (α) and the optional element of structure is called beta (β). Thus:

> *When he comes, tell him to eat his lunch*   structure: $\beta\alpha$
> *He'll be in tomorrow, if he's free*   structure: $\alpha\beta$
> *I didn't come because he told me*   structure: $\alpha\beta$
> *Harry, who had never been before, didn't know*   structure: $\alpha\langle\langle\beta\rangle\rangle$

It is obvious that independent clauses operate at α and dependent clauses at β; and that the possible sequence or inclusion of elements of sentence structure is as stated above for conditioning dependent clauses, additioning dependent clauses and reported dependent clauses. Thus, if we symbolise, β^1 = conditioning, β^2 = additioning, β^3 = reported, β^1 may precede, follow or be included in α:

When in doubt, shout out   structure: $\beta^1\alpha$

Shout out when in doubt   structure: $\alpha\beta^1$

John, if you ask him nicely, will help   structure: $\alpha\langle\langle\beta^1\rangle\rangle$

If you ask him nicely, John will help   structure: $\beta^1\alpha$

John will help, if you ask him nicely   structure: $\alpha\beta^1$

β^2 may follow or be included in α; it may not precede α:

My uncle, who is a sailor, brings presents home   structure: $\alpha\langle\langle\beta^2\rangle\rangle$

Central Africa, which is very hot, is not for me   structure: $\alpha\langle\langle\beta^2\rangle\rangle$

I like summer, when the days are long   structure: $\alpha\beta^2$

I went to Aberdeen, which is in the North   structure: $\alpha\beta^2$

β^3 with an introductory adjunct cannot precede α; it may precede α if it does not have an introductory adjunct; it cannot be included in α:

She said that she would come   structure: $\alpha\beta^3$

She said she would come   structure: $\alpha\beta^3$

She would come, she said   structure: $\beta^3\alpha$

The sentences so far considered have all been two-clause sentences, and it may seem that α and β are merely alternative names for independent and dependent clauses, since each α element has so far consisted of one independent clause, and each β element has consisted of one dependent clause. But this is the position at any rank when an element of structure is realised minimally; if (say) a P element in clause structure is realised by a verbal group with only an *l* element then verbal group and verb will be coterminous, but we could have other elements of structure in the verbal group, and we could have a number of linked verbal groups at P, as in

N	V	&	V	N
He	*washed*	*and*	*polished*	*the car*

(*Cf.* He washed,//and polished the car)

or linked *nominal groups* at S, as in

	S		
N	N	&	N
Tom,	*Mary*	*and*	*Bill*	*went out.*

If we consider sentences with more than two clauses, such as

(i) *I stayed in and read a book because I had nowhere to go and no one to see*

(ii) *If Tom comes and I'm not back, tell him to wait*

we find the same position in sentence structure. Sentence (i) contains four clauses, independent + independent + dependent + dependent. But the structure of the sentence is not merely a concatenation of clauses. The two independent clauses are linked by *and* and by omission of s in the second. What we have, in fact, is one α element consisting of two clauses, just as in:

N & N
John and Jim | *went out*

we have one s consisting of two linked nominal groups. The analysis should therefore be:

α

Ind	&	Ind
I stayed in	*and*	*read a book*

structure: α (Ind & Ind)

The two dependent clauses are also linked, and there is omission of the binding adverbial group and s in the second. The analysis should be:

β

Dep	&	Dep
because I had nothing else to do	*and*	*no one to see*

structure: β (Dep & Dep)

The analysis of the sentence is therefore

⋛

α		
Ind	&	Ind
I stayed in	*and*	*read a book*

β		
Dep	&	Dep
because I had nothing else to do	*and*	*no one to see*

We are, however, already involved in problems of linkage and ellipsis, and it may be profitable to digress at this point in order to discuss these briefly.

F

Linkage (i.e. 'coordination') poses two questions for the analyst: what items are linked? and what is the structural status of the linker?

There are two types of linkage in English. In the sentences:

I don't know, in fact, what he is going to do

We could, therefore, keep it going for quite a time

We all sent presents, nevertheless

the items *in fact, therefore, nevertheless* link the sentences to what has gone before. These are called sentence linkers. Typical realisations are *consequently, therefore, finally, however, nevertheless, so, thus, then.* This type of linker does not present many problems. There are two important points to be made about them: (i) their position is not fixed in clause structure, thus:

However, I don't think we should go on with it.

I don't think, however, that we should go on with it

I don't think we should go on with it, however;

(ii) these linkers do not allow what is usually called 'branching'; this means the formation of a sentence with linked clauses. Thus:

He therefore disagreed ⋛
$\quad\quad\quad\quad\quad\quad\quad\quad\quad$ |
$\quad\quad\quad\quad\quad\quad\quad\quad\quad$ Cl

Consequently, he disagreed ⋛
$\quad\quad\quad\quad\quad\quad\quad\quad\quad$ |
$\quad\quad\quad\quad\quad\quad\quad\quad\quad$ Cl

Such items can be regarded as realising an adjunct element in clause structure, and if desired can be superscripted A^{Link} to distinguish them from other adjuncts.

The second type of linkage, realised by the linkers *and, or, but,* is quite different. The position of these linkers is fixed and they permit 'branching', thus:

$$\overset{\displaystyle⋛}{\bigwedge}$$

I came in and he went out   Cl   Cl

$$\overset{\displaystyle⋛}{\bigwedge}$$

John played well but Mary was off form   Cl   Cl

It is with this type of linker that problems are encountered. First, their status as constituents: if two clauses are linked in the above sentences, they are both linked. It is quite arbitrary to say that the *and* belongs to either the first or the second—any two concatenated items stand in the same relation to the concatenating item. But if we decide on a ternary division of such sentences, e.g.

Ind		Ind
I came in	*and*	*John went out*

what is the status of *and*? One of the requirements of the theory on which systemic grammar is based is that all items should be accounted for at all ranks, with nothing left over. Thus the description

> *John shot Jim* → one sentence, one clause, SPC, NVM, *hlh*, noun verb noun, base base base,

accounts for every item at all ranks with nothing left over. If we apply this to *I came in and John went out* we have clauses *I came in*, *John went out*; but we have *and* left over. If we are required to account for this item at this (sentence) rank, then it will need to be a clause. This is a consequence which is surely counter-intuitive and undesirable. There is, in addition, a further problem: such linkers may link items at any rank; and this means that we should be required to treat linkers as realisations of units at each rank. Thus:

> *I play chess and he plays draughts   and =* clause
> *I play good chess and poor draughts   and =* group
> *I play good and interesting chess   and =* word
> *Fish and chips are good   and =* morpheme.

And in all of this we would have said nothing general about the function of *and*, which is surely the same in all examples.

It seems, in fact, that linkers should not be regarded as constituents in structure at all, but as realisation of a rank-free system of linkage. It means in this case that where linkage occurs this is marked (&) but not accorded constituent status. Thus:

> *I came in and John went out*   structure: Ind Cl & Ind Cl
> *big fish and little fish*   structure: nom grp & nom grp
> *fresh and bright*   structure: epithet & epithet
> *fish 'n chips*   base & base

If we now consider a sentence such as:

> *I stayed in and read a book because I had nothing to do and no one to see but John went into town to see a friend.*
> the analysis is

$\lessgtr$

α		
Ind	&	Ind
I stayed in	*and*	*read a book*

β			
Dep		&	Dep
because I had nothing to do		*and*	*no one to see*

&	α		β
	Ind		Dep
but	*John went into town*		*to see a friend.*

Two points are evident from such an analysis: (i) clauses are not merely strings of coordinated or subordinated clauses; clauses operate at elements of sentence structure, the analysis

$$\lessgtr \longrightarrow \alpha\beta \ \& \ \alpha\beta$$

reflects the structure of the sentence better than

$$\lessgtr \longrightarrow Ind \ \& \ Ind \ Dep \ \& \ Dep \ \& \ Ind \ Dep.$$

(ii) it is evident that within one *alpha* element ellipsis of s is possible:

    I stayed and read a book

and within one *beta* element ellipsis of binding adjunct and subject is possible:

    because I had nothing to do and no one to see.

And it can be seen from such examples that a clause cannot always be identified as operating at *alpha* or *beta* by its own structure. The clause

    I had no one to see

is a dependent clause at *beta* in a linked series of dependent clauses at *beta* in:

    because I had nothing to do and I had no one to see,

but is an independent clause operating at *alpha* in:

    (i) *I had nothing to do that day, and no one to see* (linked series)

    (ii) *I had no one to see* (simple sentence)

We might say that the s of the first clause in a linked series at *alpha* or *beta* is the s of the *alpha* or *beta* element, and the binder in the first *beta* clause is the binder of the *beta* element. When we change s or binder we have a new element of sentence structure. Thus:

⋛

	α	
Ind	&	Ind
I came in	and	read a book.

but

⋛

α	&	α
Ind		Ind
I came in	and	John went out.

⋛

β		α
Dep	& Dep	Ind
If I'm out	*and he phones,*	*give him a message.*

but

β	β	α
Dep	Dep	Ind
If I'm out	*when he phones,*	*give him a message.*

It might seem unnecessary to separate the dependent clauses in this last example (if all conditioning, all additioning, all reported clauses constitute elements of sentence structure); but it is not the case that *if* and *when* are exactly the same conditioning. Since the depth of the clauses is important (we cannot reverse these without an intonation break), this suggests that we have two conditioning elements, two beta elements, rather than two clauses at one beta element.

MINOR SENTENCES

Sentences which do not contain an independent clause which contains a P element in their structure may be classed as minor sentences; such sentences will be realised by moodless or dependent clauses. Minor sentences are sometimes added, as a class, to the 'statement, question, command' contextual classification of sentences. It seems, however, that a morphological classification of minor as a sentence which does not contain an independent clause with a P element is more valid, easier to apply and allows for the fact that most minor sentences can be assigned to a contextual class, though this necessitates the addition of an 'exclamatory' class. Thus:

Shoot! command
On Saturday? question
Blast it! exclamation
Next week. statement.

There are three main types of minor sentence in English, for which the usual names are:

(i) completive sentence
(ii) exclamatory sentence
(iii) aphoristic sentence.

(i) The first is called completive in the sense that it completes the cotext (the surrounding language) or the context (the relevant situation). Such completive sentences occur typically as answers to questions and additional comment to previous statements, or as situational comments such as introductions, directions, instructions. Such sentences are like major sentences in that they form an open set, which means that new instances can be produced at will, and they have intonation patterns like major sentences. They exhibit relationships with other sentences in the discourse. Thus:

(Who did it?)   *John.*
(Is it true?)   *Yes/no/perhaps.*
(When is it?)   *On Tuesday. Next week. After dinner.*
(Introduction)   *Mr. Black. Mr. White. The Jones boys.*
(Titles)   *West Side Story. East of Eden.*
(Directions)   *Straight down the street and across the bridge.*

(ii) Exclamatory sentences also have the characteristics of an open class, but do not incur relationships with other parts of the discourse. Such sentences are usually divided into primary interjections such as

Ouch! Gee! Whew! Blast! Hi.
Gosh. Golly. Hello.

and secondary interjections in which there is more than one element, such as

dear me. bless you. thank you.
blast it. good heavens. by thunder.

A third type of exclamatory sentence is the verbless equational sentence such as:

John a manager!
Thompson a first team man?

(iii) Aphoristic sentences differ from the previous types in that they form a virtually closed class. They are traditional expressions, and the native speaker is not normally at liberty to coin new examples. They operate, however, as full sentences. Thus

The more the merrier.
Least said soonest mended.
One man one vote.

ANALYSIS OF MINOR SENTENCES

Minor sentences which are realised by moodless clauses have either nominal groups or adverbial groups as constituents; since there is no P element by which s/c relations may be established the nominal groups can be regarded as realising the element z in clause structure, and all adverbial groups can be regarded as realising the element A in clause structure. This means that we are identifying the constituents morphologically, and correlating as far as possible with their normal syntactic operation in clause structure. Thus:

z	z		z	z
John	the captain!		The more	the merrier.

z		z	z
e *e* *h*		*h*	*h*
West Side Story.		*Joe Smith.*	*Gosh!*

A	A	A
p *c*	*p* *c*	*p* *c*
On [Tuesday.]	*About [nine.]*	*For [a minute.]*

Minor sentences which have dependent clause(s) as constituents will, of course, have normal clause analysis. Thus:

	A	S	P
(When are we going?)	*When*	*John*	*returns.*

Minor sentences are frequent in some types of literary work. These will obviously be considered as completive sentences, but this does not mean that they should be analysed by 'supplying' (finite) verbal or (subject) nominal elements. They occur in the text as minor sentences, and the fact that they do has obvious stylistic ramifications. It is therefore not proper to treat them as 'elliptic/fragmented' sentences and suggest that the 'full' form must be accounted for.

Two short extracts may illustrate the point:

(i) Fog everywhere. Fog up the river, where it flows among green aits and meadows; fog down the river, where it rolls defiled among the tiers of shipping, and the waterside pollutions of a great (and dirty) city. Fog on the Essex marshes, fog on the Kentish heights. Fog creeping into the cabooses of collier-brigs ... Verdict accordingly. Accidental death. No doubt. Good afternoon.
(C. Dickens: *Bleak House.*)

(ii) It looked like a miniature bank. A short counter. A grilled window protected by burglar proof plastic.
 . . . and there was a travel office! A sure out.
(A. Bester: *The Demolished Man.*)

The various minor sentences realised by moodless and dependent clauses must be analysed as discussed above, e.g.

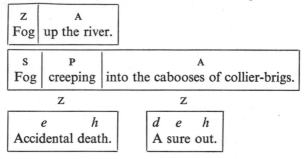

Z	A
Fog	up the river.

S	P	A
Fog	creeping	into the cabooses of collier-brigs.

Z			Z		
e		*h*	*d*	*e*	*h*
Accidental death.			A sure out.		

RANKSHIFT

Some discussion and illustration of rankshifting have already been entered into in the previous pages. It may be of value to consider rankshift as a separate aspect, and to illustrate again the main types of rankshift which occur.

The theory on which the model of description is based allows for a downward rankshift. This means that a unit which normally operates in the structure of the next highest unit (and this is a crucial criterion in the definition of units) may also operate in the structure of a lower unit or in the structure of a unit of the same rank. A unit so operating is said to be rankshifted.

Clause is that unit which operates at elements of sentence structure; but it has been shown that clause may also operate at q in nominal group structure. Group is that unit which operates at elements of clause structure; but it has been shown that groups may also operate at q in other groups, and at d in other groups.

There are, in fact, five main types of rankshift which occur in English, and it may be useful to illustrate these separately.

1 Clause rankshifted to operate at q in nominal group structure:
  (i) With finite verbal group at P:
  (a) *who, which*
      The man [*who came to dinner*] *stayed a month*
      The box [*which he thought most suitable*] *was already taken*
  (b) *where, when, why*
      The place [*where John lived*] *was Paris*
      The day [*when they were married*] *was Tuesday*
      The reason [*why they left*] *was the lateness of the hour*
  (c) *that*
      The colour [*that I like*] *is red*
  (d) ——
      The boy [*you like*] *is here*
  (ii) With non-finite verbal group at P:
  (a) infinitival: *The person* [*to ask*] *is John*
  (b) participial: *The room* [*facing South*] *is cold.*

2 Clause rankshifted to operate as whole nominal group (nominal clause):
  (i) With finite verbal group at P:
  (a) *who, which*
      [*Who the man was*] *is a mystery*
      The results showed which theory was right
  (b) *where, when, why, how*
      [*Where the river bends*] *is a nice spot*
      Tuesday was [*when his plan worked*]
      [*How (why) John's plan works*] *is important*
  (c) *that*
      [*That he should sing*] *is an outrage*
  (ii) With non-finite verbal group at P:
  (a) infinitival: *I like* [*to be left alone*]
  (b) participial: [*Driving fast*] *is what I like*
                   [*Running a race*] *is good fun*
                   John is [*a man driven crazy*].

3 Adverbial group rankshifted to operate at *q* in nominal group structure:

> *The houses [by the river] will not last long.*

In the identification of this rankshift, care must be taken to distinguish between rankshifted adverbial group at *q* and non-rankshifted adverbial group at A in clause structure, thus:

S	P		C
I	*bought*		*the house [by the river]*

S	P	C	A
I	*left*	*my clothes*	*by the river.*

4 Nominal group rankshifted to operate at *d* in nominal group structure:

> *[The town council]'s houses*
> *[The house on the hill]'s four green doors.*

5 Nominal group rankshifted to operate at *c* in an adverbial group:

> p   c
> *by [the river]*
> p   c
> *up [the hill]*

In an example such as

> *The houses by the river are to be sold*

the nominal group *the river* is rankshifted to *c* in the adverbial group *by the river*, and the adverbial group *by the river* is rankshifted to *q* in the nominal group *The houses by the river*. We obviously have double rankshift, thus:

m	*h*		*q* = [Ad]
		p	*c* = [N]
The	*houses*	*[by*	*[the river]] . . .*

If the nominal group *the river* had itself a further *q* element this would involve multiple rankshift, a feature of some English registers.

SENTENCE ANALYSIS

It is evident from previous illustrations that the analysis of a sentence (or of any other unit) may be presented in the form of a 'box' analysis as in Figure 3 or a 'tree' analysis as in Figure 4.

There are, of course, various ways of presenting analyses; the chief virtues of the two methods mentioned are that they show the step-by-step description down the rankscale, and that they preserve the sequence of the text. This means that we do not get (as in some 'column' analysis) a sentence analysis presented as

soldiers	the	impaled	on sharpened stakes	prisoners	their
	heedless of their pain				

for *The soldiers, heedless of their pain, impaled their prisoners on sharpened stakes.*

The 'tree' type of presentation also facilitates comparison of sentences, and measurement of the relative complexity of sentences, since the number of branching 'nodes' will be a reflection of the complexity of the sentence and in particular of the amount of rank-shifting involved. It is also possible to curtail the analysis at any point on the rankscale, and the analysis will be valid and comprehensive to that point; we may for example wish to analyse to clause rank, thus:

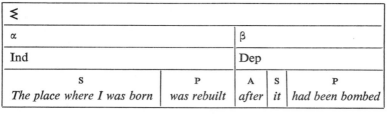

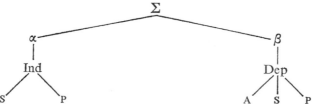

Some illustration of these types of presentation of analysis is given in Figures 5–9, using the following sentences as examples:

Simple {
(i) *He struck a blow.*
(ii) *All the boys called him a good player.*
(iii) *In the evening, Tom and Dick will visit the man who lives there.*

Compound
{
  (iv) *When he comes, give me a ring.*
  (v) *The company, who now employ seventy persons, hope that work will begin at once and that the factory will be ready in time.*
}

FIGURE 3

α							
Ind							
S		P	C		A		
N		V	N		Ad		
d	*h*	*l*	*d*	*h*	*p*	*c* [N]	
det	noun	verb	det	noun	prep	*d* det	*h* noun
The	*dog*	*bit*	*the*	*boy*	*in*	*the*	*arm*

FIGURE 4

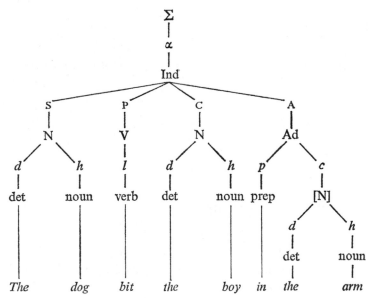

FIGURE 5

(i) *He struck a blow.*

≶

α			
Ind			
S	P	C^E	
N	V	N	
h	*l*	*d*	*h*
pron *He*	verb *struck*	det *a*	noun *blow.*

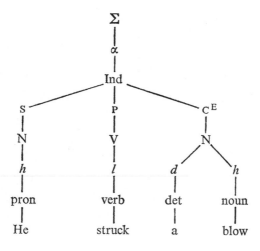

FIGURE 6

(ii) *All the boys called him a good player.*

α							
Ind							
S			P	C^E	C^I		
N			V	N	N		
d_1	d_2	h	l	h	d	e	h
det	det	noun	verb	pron	det	adj	noun
All	*the*	*boys*	*called*	*him*	*a*	*good*	*player.*

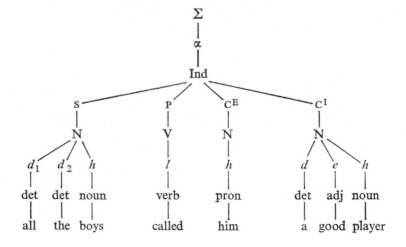

FIGURE 7

(iii) *In the evening, Tom and Dick will visit the man who lives there.*

≤												
α												
Ind												
A			**S**			**P**		**C^E**				
Ad			N	&	N	V		N				
p	*c*		*h*		*h*	*a*	*l*	*d*	*h*	*q*		
prep			pr noun		pr noun	aux	verb	det	noun	[[Cl]]		
										S	P	A
	[N]									N	V	Ad
	d	*h*								*h*	*l*	*a*
	det	noun								rel	verb	adv
In	the	evening	Tom	and	Dick	will	visit	the	man	who	lives	there

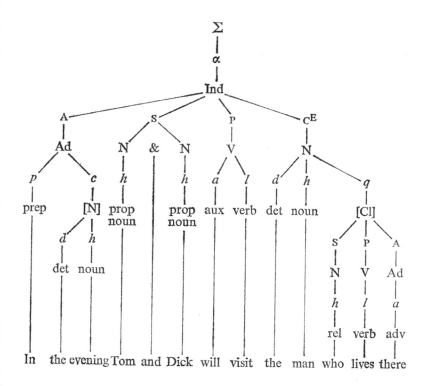

FIGURE 8

(iv) *When he comes, give me a ring.*

⋚						
β			α			
Dep			Ind			
A	S	P	P	C^E	C^E	
Ad	N	V	V	N	N	
a	*h*	*l*	*l*	*h*	*d*	*h*
adv	pron	verb	verb	pron	det	noun
When	*he*	*comes*	*give*	*me*	*a*	*ring.*

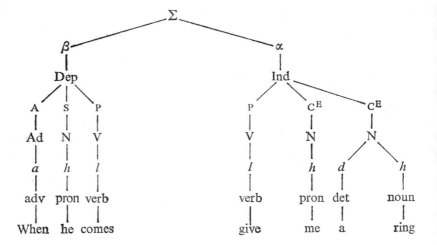

G

FIGURE 9

(v) *The company, who now employ seventy persons, hope that work will begin at once and that the empty factory will be ready in time.*

W	The	company,	who	now	employ	seventy	persons,	hope	that	work	will	begin	at	once	and	that	the	factory	will	be	ready	in	time
α / β	α								β														
Ind / Dep / & / Dep	Ind		Dep					«β»	Dep						&	Dep							
Function	s		s	A	P	c^E		P	A	s	P		A			A	s		P		c^I	A	c
Category	N		N	Ad	V	N		V	Ad	N	V			Ad		Ad	N		V		N		[N]
														[N]									
Letter	d	h	h	e	l	o	h	l	q	h	q	l	p	h		a	d	h	q	l	h	p	h
Part of speech	det	noun	rel	adv	verb	numeral	noun	verb	adv	noun	aux	verb	prep	noun	and	adv	det	noun	aux	verb	adj	prep	noun
Word	The	company,	who	now	employ	seventy	persons,	hope	that	work	will	begin	at	once	and	that	the	factory	will	be	ready	in	time

See overleaf for continuation of Figure 9.

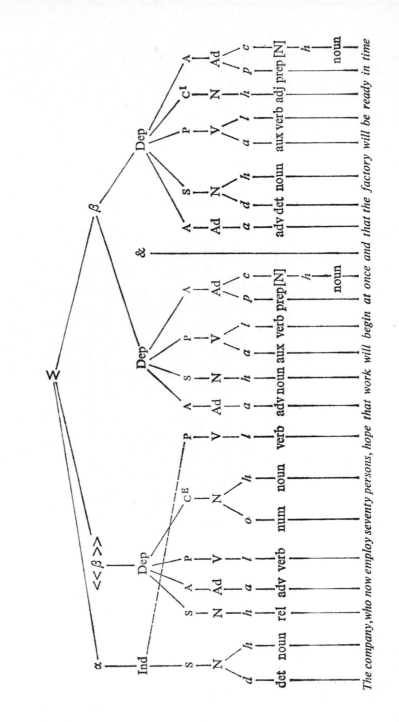

3
Deep Grammar

Part 2 was intended to provide a description of the occurring patterns of English sentences. Two points regarding the inadequacy of this description were made in the General Survey:

(i) similar descriptions will be given to unrelated sentences, as
> *This coat buttons easily*   structure: SPA
> *This knife cuts easily*   structure: SPA

and dissimilar descriptions will be given to related sentences, as
> *John shot Jim*   structure: SPC
> *Jim was shot by John*   structure: SPA;

(ii) the description will not show what else may have occurred at any particular place, i.e. from what set of possibilities the particular occurrence was selected; for example: that a nominal group *the boy* represents a choice of singular from the set of possibilities singular/plural, that a verbal group *bites* represents the choice present from the set of possibilities present/past/future.

A further point may be made. Sentences such as *It was John who read the book* present some difficulties for analysis. The simplest analysis would seem to be:

S	P	C
It	*was*	*John who read the book.*

But this involves awkwardness in the further analysis of C: *John* is a proper noun and as such would not be expected to have a *q* element, which would seem to be the only possibility for *who read the book*. Usually *It* is said to be a 'dummy' subject and the 'real' subject is

John. This explanation is well motivated; it certainly seems that a description which assigns *John* to subject function is desired. The explanation of 'dummy' and 'real' subject goes part of the way towards explaining such structures, but does not show the relatedness of this sentence to other sentences, such as:

John read the book.
The book John read (*but not the play*).
The book was read by John.

It must be shown that the original sentence was a choice from a number of possibilities, a set called 'theme' below.

The set of possibilities available at any place specified by the surface grammar is called a system, and the individual choices are called terms or features in the system. Thus:

System	*Terms*	*Environment* ('*place on the chain*')
Number ⟶	⌈Singular ⌊Plural	Subject/Complement
Tense ⟶	⌈Present ⊢Past ⌊Future	Predicator
Mood ⟶	⌈Indicative ⌊Imperative	Major Clause

There are two points to be noted about systems:

(i) We need to specify the place of operation, the environment on the chain, before we specify the choices available there: the assignment of systems presupposes the surface grammar already discussed. Nevertheless, it may prove desirable to give a systemic description, a feature specification, of expressions from which structure may be derived rather than the other way round. This is because structurally similar descriptions may be the realisation of different combinations of systemic features, but systemic descriptions are unique. This point is illustrated in the following sections.

(ii) Some systems are dependent on selection from other systems; only verbal groups which have already chosen finite in the system of finiteness can make a further choice from the system of modality; selection of a term in the system of theme at clause rank is only available after selection from the system of mood. There is, therefore, a hierarchy of systems. The principle of 'deep' and 'surface' grammar is evident in traditional formulations; when it is said that a clause is 'indicative, finite' etc., or a verb is 'finite, present, active' etc., this means that a place 'clause/verb' is the point of origin for the choices 'indicative, finite/present, active'. This is not, however, made explicit; neither is the dependency of choices on prior choices. We need to know two things: (i) what other choices were possible at the same place, and (ii) what the 'entry requirement' was, i.e. what previous selection or selections was or were necessary before this choice was possible.

A full systemic description of English is not yet available. Clause and group are ranks where systems are numerous and important. A description of the most prominent systems in these environments is given below.

It is perhaps appropriate to mention here the further implications of the term 'Introduction' in the title of this book. The following brief discussion explains what this book is intended to introduce.

It becomes increasingly evident that the grammar of a language, at its deepest level, is concerned with the organisation of systems of choices which contrast with each other, and which are therefore mutually exclusive and mutually defining. At this level the question of choice is a question of choice between different meanings.

These meaningful choices are related to the classes and structures of surface grammar by a scale of realisation. Each systemic term specifies a structural component: thus, the feature 'indicative' specifies that the element s will occur in clause structure; the term 'declarative' will further specify the sequence SP in clause structure; the term 'operative' will specify the presence of a C element in clause structure.

Thus we can say that the feature selection: 'indicative; declarative; operative' is realised in clause structure as SPC.

The structures of language are themselves functional; they occur as they do because that is how they achieve effective communication. These functions have been designated experiential, interpersonal and textual.

The functions of language may perhaps be most broadly and generally expressed as 'meaning', 'mood' and 'message'.

Meaning in this sense is concerned with matters of experience (whether 'real' or not), and is most clearly related to the transitivity systems, to the participants and processes involved. Mood in this sense is concerned with the speaker's role (questioning, stating, commanding, etc.), and is clearly related to the mood and modality systems, but also to the modal operation of certain adjuncts. Message in this sense is concerned with the distribution of information points and highlights throughout the discourse, and is most clearly related to the theme and information systems (though the scope of such systems is only touched upon in this book). Halliday has designated these functions of language 'experiential, interpersonal and textual'.

The components of a grammar must be related to these functions of language. This is shown in Figure 10.

FIGURE 10

	Experiential	*Interpersonal*	*Textual*
Clause	Transitivity: process, participants, circumstantial elements, polarity	Mood: types of speech function; modality; tone	Theme: identification, predication, substitution of theme
Verbal group	Verb classes: tense	Modality; marked polarity	Voice; contrast; substitution and ellipsis
Nominal group	Noun and adjective classes; modifying functions —epithet, quantifier, possessive	Modification intensification	Deixis and anaphora; pronouns; comparison; substitution; ellipsis.

For further exemplification and description see the following articles by M. A. K. Halliday: 'Functional Diversity in Language as seen from a consideration of Modality and Mood in English' in *Foundations of Language Vol. 6*, 1970; 322–361; and 'Language Structure and Language Function' in *New Horizons in Linguistics* ed. John Lyons, 1970; 140–165.

3.1   *Systems at Clause Rank*

Any clause which is major and independent must select from the systems of mood, theme, transitivity and information which are discussed individually in the following sections.

3.1.1   *Mood*

There are two points to be noted initially about this system:

(i) it is not to be confused with modality, which is a system whose environment is the verbal group, and whose features are realised by modal verbs;

(ii) traditionally, features of mood (or, more precisely, the realisation of features of mood) are assigned to a form of the verb, and a clause containing such a verbal form is said to express a 'statement, question, command' according to which form of the verb occurs.

It is evident from the earlier discussion of verbal inflexion that a 'form of the verb' will not itself indicate features of mood; thus, *take* is said to realise the imperative mood of the verb *take*, but does not differ from the base form of the verb in any of its various functions. Semantic definitions which rely on interpretation of clauses as 'statement, question, command' and so on are more appropriate to sentence rank, and certainly some more formal indication of features will be expected at clause rank. There are sentences which might reasonably be interpreted as 'commands' but which may not contain what we want to call an imperative clause. There seems little point in talking about 'indicative, subjunctive, imperative' moods of the verb, and then saying that the one verbal form *take* realises all three features. It seems clear that features of mood are realised at clause rank, not at verb or sentence rank: the mood features are realised, in fact, by particular arrangements of (some of) the elements of clause structure; and features of mood are not in a one-to-one relation with contextual classes of sentence. If we consider the clauses

    (i) *John comes*

    (ii) *Is John coming?*

    (iii) *Come*

we see that (i) and (ii) have a s element but (iii) does not. Clauses which contain a s are called indicative, clauses which do not contain a s are called imperative. The first choice in the mood system may thus be represented:

$$\text{Mood} \longrightarrow \left[\begin{array}{l}\text{Indicative}\\\text{Imperative}\end{array}\right.$$

This, of course, is to beg the question of subjects in imperative clauses. Traditionally it is said the second person pronoun (*you*) is —overtly or covertly—present in all imperative clauses, and is the subject of such clauses. The evidence for this point of view can be presented very convincingly. Referring to this problem, O. Jespersen (1940; Vol 3: 224) states:

> A subject may be added, chiefly to give emotional colouring to the imperative; often with some emphasis on the pronoun (and with a pointing gesture).

This type of clause is exemplified by:

You, come here
Come here, you.

Elsewhere, (1940; Vol 5: 467) Jespersen states:

> We frequently find the imperative with a third person subject. Sometimes this may be considered a vocative, as manifested by the comma which modern editors insert.

This type of clause is exemplified by:

Come here, somebody
Somebody, come here.

Jespersen seems correct in adducing 'vocative' and in drawing attention to the comma. He seems less correct in stating such elements may 'sometimes' be regarded as vocatives (how do we define 'sometimes'?) and in calling them subjects. They are certainly nominal groups, and may be as complex structurally as any nominal group. They are clearly not complements, and so may indeed be considered as subjects at first. But they do not behave like other subjects, in that:

(i) they are often (and may be always) separated from the rest of the clause by a comma in the written language and an intonation break in the spoken language. As in

Boys, stop playing when it gets dark
(*cf. Boys stop playing when it gets dark*).

(ii) Not only may such an element be separated from the rest of the clause in this way, but also it may appear in clause-final position. As in

Stop playing when it gets dark, boys
(*cf.* **Stop playing when it gets dark boys*).

(iii) Since imperative clauses cannot occur with certain ('past-time') adverbial groups, there is no possibility of an imperative interpretation of:

Mother let us go to the pictures last night
(*cf. Mother, let us go to the pictures tonight*)

And because of restriction on 'place' adjuncts, there is no likelihood of an imperative interpretation of:

Boys stop playing when it gets dark in China.

It seems best to consider such nominal groups as vocative elements; if anything is consistently present in imperative clauses it is the feature vocative. The realisation of imperative is absence of subject, and possible presence of a z vocative (z^{voc}) element in clause structure.

The initial choice in the mood system is thus between indicative and imperative. If a clause is indicative, there is a further choice to be made between declarative and interrogative. A declarative clause has its subject preceding its predicator, as in:

S | P
John | *is coming*

S | P | C
The centre | *scored* | *three goals*

S | P | C
He | *was called* | *a saint.*

An interrogative clause has either the subject included in the predicator, or an initial WH element (i.e. who, which, where, when, why, how), or both, as in:

P-- S --P
Is John coming?

A | P-- | S | --P | C
When | *will* | *that centre* | *score* | *a goal?*

S | P | C
Who | *will be* | *the first to dive?*

The Mood system may now be represented:

Mood ——→ [Indicative ——————→ [Declarative / Interrogative] ; Imperative]

It is obvious that interrogative clauses may be either WH interrogatives or non-WH interrogatives. This distinction might alternatively be labelled (as it often is) 'yes/no' or 'non-yes/no' interrogatives. In non-WH interrogatives it is the polarity (p. 137) which is in question, the 'yes-ness or no-ness' of the clause, and the predicted answer is 'yes' or 'no'. In WH interrogatives it is not the polarity which is in question, and the answer is not predictable in any generalised sense.

Further, in WH interrogatives it may be the identification of the subject which is in question or it may be some other element. If it is the former then the WH element is the subject of the clause, and takes the initial clause position usual for WH elements (not the included s position for interrogatives), as in *Who will be the first to dive?* If it is not the subject of the clause which is in question the WH element will take initial position in the clause and the s will be included in the p, as in *When will he score a goal? Where shall we find another one?* The Mood system may now, and finally, be represented:

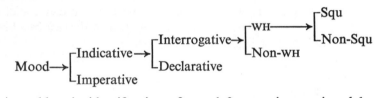

A problem in identification of mood features is occasioned by clauses such as *Here come my friends.* In this clause the nominal group *my friends* would appear to be subject, since a change of number from plural to singular will necessitate concord with the verbal group at P: *Here comes my friend.* Such clauses could be considered a special type of declarative clause, marked by the presence of the (unstressed) introductory adjunct. However, such clauses occur without any introductory adjunct: *said John.* The main difference between interrogative clauses and declarative clauses is that the former have subject included in the predicator, the latter have subject preceding the predicator; but if there is only one item realising the verbal group at P then it is not possible to show the distinction. There would seem to be possible ambiguity of mood features. That is, a clause such as *has John* may, on what has so far been considered, be either declarative or interrogative. It is obviously necessary to distinguish between PS declaratives and PS interrogatives. The mood feature realisation depends on the item realising the verbal group: if the item is an auxiliary verb then the clause is interrogative; if the item is a lexical verb then the clause is declarative. Since PS interrogatives contain only an auxiliary verb their occurrence will be restricted in the same way as the occurrence of non-interrogative clauses with only an auxiliary verb in the verbal group i.e. will be a case of substitution (pp. 42–43). We may therefore incorporate the description of these PS interrogatives in the description of *auxiliaries*, and consider other PS *clauses* as *declarative*. We can now say that the feature *declarative* is realised by either SP or PS in *clause structure*, the feature *interrogative* is realised by PSP in clause structure, and the feature *imperative* is realised by P with no S in *clause structure*. The following pairs of clauses differ in only one mood feature, whatever their differences in surface structure:

A	B
John comes	*John, come*
indicative	imperative
The centre scored a goal	*Did the centre score a goal?*
indicative: declarative	indicative: interrogative
Who broke the window?	*Is the window broken?*
indicative: interrogative: WH	indicative: interrogative: non-WH
When did he buy the book?	*Who bought the book?*
indicative: interrogative: WH: non-Squ	indicative: interrogative: WH: Squ.

3.1.2 *Theme*

The preceding section was concerned with presence or absence of S in clause structure, and with the various arrangements of S and P as realisations of terms in the mood system. The position of A in clause structure was discussed previously (pp. 63 *ff*.). The presence or absence of C in clause structure is determined by the transitivity systems, to be discussed in the next section; for the moment we may say that if a C is present in clause structure it usually occupies the position immediately after P. In other words, apart from 'binding' adjuncts—*if*, *because*, etc., and linkers—*and*, *or*—which are all fixed in position and are not relevant to the theme system, we can say that the usual order for elements of structure in a declarative clause is S P C A. It is not the case, however, that this order of elements is fixed in English; only that it is being taken as the most normal. We can regard this as neutral or unmarked, and contrast other permitted sequences against this norm. What is called the thematic element in a clause is the first element which results from choice (i.e. excludes the binders and linkers mentioned above, since their position is fixed, and not a matter of choice).

We can, therefore, distinguish between clauses unmarked for theme, and clauses which are marked for theme. An unmarked theme will be realised by having the mood exponents in initial position; a declarative clause, for example, which has s in initial position is unmarked for theme. A clause which has an element other than a mood exponent in initial position will be marked for theme. The primary distinction in the theme system is thus:

$$\text{Theme} \longrightarrow \begin{bmatrix} \text{Marked} \\ \text{Unmarked.} \end{bmatrix}$$

We may now proceed to consider what different types of marked theme occur in English.

The c in clause structure normally follows P, and if no A is present it is clause-final. But the c may occur in clause-initial position. Such structures are usually discussed in terms of 'inversion'; this name is appropriate if it means inversion of the most usual order in English; but if it is taken to mean (as it sometimes seems to be) that there is some 'breaking' or 'extending' of grammatical rules involved it is clearly inappropriate. It is often said that English word order is fixed, but when examples are given to illustrate the point it is obvious that it is not 'words' that are meant, but elements of clause structure —SPC. The elements of clause structure are variable in sequence, and it is precisely because they are variable that values can be given to certain sequences in contrast to other sequences which might have occurred.

Clauses with initial c are perfectly grammatical in English. Thus:

C	S	P	A
Football	*I'*	*ll play*	*anytime*

C	S	P	A
Him	*the almighty power*	*hurled*	*headlong*

C	S	P
These papers	*you*	*can have* (but leave those).

These clauses have marked theme, marked by initial position of C. This is called c-theme (thematic C).

The possibility of A-theme is similar. The 'lexical' adjuncts which usually occur at position 3 (p. 64) can occur in initial position in clause structure. The clause is marked for theme by this position of adjunct. Thus:

> *On a former occasion we had discussed this* ⎫
> *In the evening, we went down to the beach to play* ⎬ ASP
> *Never has so much been owed* ⎪
> *On the occasion of this anniversary, we drink to . . .* ⎭

The third of these examples shows that position 2 adjuncts can also be thematic, and when they are the subject of the clause it is included in the predicator; other examples are:

> *Seldom have I seen so poor a game*
> *Rarely did I find anything interesting there.*

This does not cause ambiguity with the included subject interrogative clause, because of the thematic adjunct marking the clause. Often a thematic A correlates with an intonation break in the spoken language, and this is reflected by the commas in the above examples.

In a declarative clause which is unmarked for theme the subject is usually 'given' in that it has already been mentioned in the text or is known in the situation. It is also usual for the tonic syllable (primary stress) in a clause to fall on the last lexical item in the clause. This is what we should expect: if the subject is 'given', is the theme of the clause, then some other element is 'new' and so receives the highlight afforded by the tonic syllable. So in the clause *John read the* book (i.e. *not the play*) (tonic 'book'), *John* is already known and *book* is the 'new' information and takes the tonic syllable. A subject can, however, be marked as 'new' information by taking the tonic syllable. John *read the book* (i.e. *not Mary or Bill*). This, indeed, is only one of the possibilities of marked tonicity (pp. 101 *ff.*); and could be included in the information systems. It seems in place here as a foregrounding of an element of clause structure similar to the foregrounding of C and A discussed above. It is also the case that s-new often correlates with the fourth, and final, term in the marked theme types: predicated theme. Some discussion was entered into above regarding the difficulty of a satisfactory analysis of *It is John who read the book*. If we consider this to be the selection of predicated theme as against non-predicated theme (i.e. *John read the book*), then we can say that it is realised in surface structure as

> *It* + '*be*' + s (of the non-P theme clause) + WH (i.e. appropriate relative) + P (of the non-P theme clause) + C (of the non-P theme clause).

And if we relate these clauses in this way they will be shown as closely related, as differing in only one systemic feature:

John read the book   indicative: declarative: non-P-theme

It was John who read the book   indicative: declarative: P-theme.

We have, therefore, four possible types of marked theme in the clause:

The theme system applies to interrogative clauses also, and declarative and interrogative clauses can be considered together in relation to theme. It may, however, be clearer to add a separate statement of interrogatives. In WH interrogative clauses, whether Squ or non-Squ, the WH element normally occurs in initial position. Thus:

Who is coming?

When is he coming?

Initial WH element is therefore unmarked for theme in interrogative clauses. An interrogative clause may be marked for theme, if either:

(a) the WH element occurs in other than initial position

or

(b) the WH element is initial but takes the tonic syllable; (this is usually called an 'echo' question, since it is a request for information to be repeated).

Thus:

You're going *where*?

Who is coming?

It is obvious that with a Squ only the latter possibility of marking is possible, since *John shot whom?* will always be interpreted as SPC. This provides an illustration of the fact that discussion of 'case' in English (by reference to the few remaining pronominal inflexions) as marking clause functions of s and c are misguided; this type of clause would be possible if even the pronominal cases were effective. We have the following possibilities of marked theme:

Unmarked   *Marked*

Whom did he *shoot*?⟶ ⎡*Whom* did he shoot?
                     ⎣He shot *whom*?

Where did he *go*?━━━━━━━━━→⌈*Where* did he go?
                               ⌊He went *where*?

Whom is presumably 'accusative' case, and marks 'object' function in the clause in contrast to its 'nominative' form (*who*) which marks subject function in the clause. *Where* is a non-inflexional adjunctival element which does not affect the point. If the uninflected 'nominative' case of *whom* did mark 'subject' then a clause such as 'Who shot John?' ought to have the same thematic possibilities as the previous examples.

Who shot *John*━━━━━━→⌈*Who* shot John?
                         ⌊(John shot *who*?)

That this is not so, that *John shot who* will always be interpreted as SPC, with *John* as 'actor' and *who* as 'goal', is a reflection of the fact that order of elements of clause structure is a stronger realisation of function in the clause than is 'case' marking.

We might diagram separately for interrogatives:

Theme
(interr.)━━━━→⌈Marked━━━━━━→⌈WH non-initial
                               ⌊WH tonic
               ⌊Unmarked

3.1.3 *Information*

Connected speech is a sequence of stretches marked by phonological breaks. A. A. Hill (*Introduction to Linguistic Structures*, New York, 1958) gives the example:

  He will act roughly, in the same manner
  He will act, roughly in the same manner,

and rightly observes that the commas in the written language reflect the occurrence of intonation breaks in the spoken language. A stretch of language between intonation breaks is a tone group.

Within any such tone group there will be one tonic syllable ('primary stress'). Thus:

  He will act *rough*ly, in the same *man*ner
  He will *act*, roughly in the same *man*ner.

Reaching over each tone group, and having its distinctive movement at the tonic syllable, is one of the possible tones in English.

There are thus three factors to be considered:

  'stretches'━━→tone groups (tonality)
  'stress'━━→tonic syllable (tonicity)
  'voice inflection'━━→tone (tone)

Such features can be established in phonology, without reference to grammar. Difficulty in linguistic description is occasioned if such features of intonation are taken to be direct exponents of grammatical units and classes. The most common statement of this kind is perhaps that one tone group = one clause. If we consider the expression *I didn't go because he told me* we know this may occur with an intonation break after *go*:

I didn't go//because he told me

or without such a break:

I didn't go because he told me//.

The difference is a meaningful difference; but it is not a difference between two clauses and one clause. In either case the sentence contains two clauses, an independent clause followed by a dependent clause. So with grammatical classes; it is often said that a 'rising tone' signals a question, i.e. an interrogative clause. However:

    (i) *Is John doing it?*
    (ii) *When will John do it?*
    (iii) *John is doing it*

may all be said with a 'falling tone', but (i) and (ii) are interrogative and (iii) is declarative.

We can consider phonologic patterns from the 'phonetic' point of view, and discover what phonological patterns are in fact available in English; or we can consider phonological patterns from the grammatical point of view, and discover what grammatical distinctions are realised by features of intonation. The latter approach is adopted here. The distinctions marked by intonation features are taken to be meaningful and to be grammatical; they are just as much formal contrasts as are those between (say) singular/plural, past/present, indicative/imperative. A full description of intonationally expounded systems would assign such distinctions to the appropriate places in the grammar; some are concerned at group level, with different classes of group, some at clause level and so on. The primary distinctions realised by tonality and tonicity are glanced at below. No attempt is made at a comprehensive description even at primary delicacy; the intention is to show how such intonationally realised choices are accommodated in the grammar (but see also nominal group structure (pp. 33 *ff.*), and the systems of contrast and focus in the verbal group systems (pp. 139 *ff.*)).

Tonality is the distribution of tone groups in an utterance; where such stretches begin and end. Tonality is obligatory in that speech will necessarily contain tone groups, but the speaker has the option as to where they will occur. There is a high correlation between tone group and clause in English—though this, as was said earlier, should not be raised to a definition of clause; indeed, it is only after a clause has been identified that such a statement is possible. This correlation can be utilised, and one tone group being coterminous with one clause can be regarded as neutral tonality. Thus:

I didn't go//because he told me.

There are then two marked possibilities; a tone group may be more than a clause or less than a clause. The former occurs frequently when a reporting followed by a reported clause occurs in sentence structure, as in:

I asked Tom how it was done//
I told him why we did it that way//.

The second possibility, tone group less than a clause, occurs frequently before adjuncts in clause structure, as in:

He had become a teacher//in defiance of his father
He will act roughly//in the same manner.

This is also very frequent with thematic adjuncts, as in:

On this great opening day//we must pay tribute to . . .
After a sumptuous meal,//we went back to the . . .

These stretches are called information units; so an information unit equal to one clause is an unmarked information unit; an information unit equal to less than or more than a clause is marked.

We can also recognise a neutral or unmarked term in tonicity. When the tonic syllable is located on the last lexical item in the clause then the tonicity is unmarked. Thus:

I meet him in the *square*

I *meet* him.

Marked tonicity occurs when the tonic falls on some other lexical item or on a clause-final grammatical item. Thus:

I meet him in the square

I meet *him*

It *may* be alright.

We can summarise this brief consideration of intonation features by saying that there is a system of information which is concerned with the distribution of information units (i.e. the location of tone groups), and with the focusing on a point of information within each such group (i.e. the location of the tonic syllable). Thus:

H

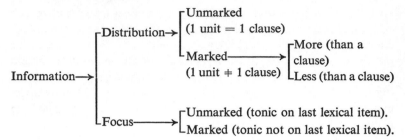

3.1.4 Transitivity[9]

On pp. 57 *ff*. the unit clause was discussed in terms of transitivity; this related to the presence or absence of the element C in clause structure. The scale-category definition of transitivity is exemplified in the following quote from Halliday:

> The terms 'intransitive, transitive' refer to clauses with no C, at least one C, one C and two C's respectively.

The main difference between this and traditional accounts is that here transitivity is being accounted for at clause rank, but traditionally it is accounted for as a feature of the verb, i.e. at word rank (or, at best, at (verbal) group rank). The traditional view, as expressed by Treble and Vallins (*An A.B.C. of English Usage*, Oxford, 1936) is:

> A verb is said to be used transitively when the action or state that it denotes is regarded as 'going over' to, i.e. as directed towards, an object. When the action or state is regarded as affecting only the subject, i.e. as not directed towards an object, the verb is called intransitive; in 'birds fly' the verb is intransitive, in 'boys fly kites' it is transitive. Many verbs can thus be used transitively or intransitively.

The difference between the approaches is not a trivial one. Considerable research work is currently being carried out on the numerous problems connected with transitivity in English. It is now recognised that the surface concept of transitivity is the environment for a network of systems. The relationships between nominal elements of clause structure (S and C) and verbal elements of clause structure (P) are various, and are realisations of relationships between 'participants' and 'processes'.

It is evident that the form of the verb alone will not indicate whether it is transitive or intransitive in Treble and Vallins' terms:

in their examples *birds fly, boys fly kites,* the identification of *fly* as transitive or intransitive is not made by reference to the form of the verb *fly*; it is necessary to observe whether or not there is a c present (an 'object' to which the action 'passes over'). Since the identification of transitivity types thus requires the recognition of clausal relations (PC or not PC) then it seems more appropriate to consider transitivity as a feature of the clause rather than a feature of the verb.

In any case, the many problems connected with what underlies such clausal relationships are not revealed by such a definition as that above. It is not, for example, evident that in
Boys fly kites
He threw the ball
He turned out a great player
quite different features are realised by the elements s and c, though all the clauses are transitive.

Consideration of such problems perhaps depends on what we want our grammar to account for; if we want a description of the physically realised events of language, the various 'states' in which we find the language, then a surface description of transitivity is perhaps sufficient. But if we want to (attempt to) account for the relations between the various 'states' of language, for what underlies the surface realisations, then something further is required.

Not only the problems posed by the different features realised (the different 'roles' fulfilled by s and c) in clauses such as
He sank the boat
He eats fish
He became a teacher,
but the fact that *He cuts easily* is interpreted differently from *He cut dexterously* and *He shaves well* is interpreted differently from *That barber shaves well* is involved in the elucidation of problems of transitivity.

It has been observed that in the clauses:[10]
(a) *John polished the table*
(b)   i. *The table polished well*
    ii. *The table was polished (by John)*
    iii. *The table was highly polished*
(a) is the exception in terms of sequence. It seems reasonable to assume that the relationship between *the table* and *polished* is constant, though in (a) *the table* is c and in (b) *the table* is s; and further,

that the relationship between *John* and *polished* is constant, though in (a) *John* is s, and in (b) ii. *John* is optionally present in an A. It follows that if *the table* and *John* are realisation of 'participants' connected with a process (*polishing*)—realised as the P of the clause— then neither of these roles is tied to any one element of clause structure.

We may summarise the argument by saying that traditional notions of 'actor–action–goal' in English clauses have good foundation, but it is important to note that we cannot generalise and say that in English s = actor, c = goal. There are other types of participants than the two above; and it is not the case with these that 'actor' is always realised as s and 'goal' is always realised as c: it is only the case that s = 'actor' and c = 'goal' in a particular type of clause, and in another type of clause the s may realise the 'goal'. What is required is an account of different English clause types according to the relationships realised by the nominal and verbal elements in clause structure.

Such an account is, in part at least, a description of the systems for which transitivity is the environment. An attempt to discuss these is given in the following pages, beginning with the more obvious distinctions and proceeding thereafter to some more delicate distinctions. The account is not intended to be comprehensive, but to illustrate and describe some of the principal options available in the transitivity systems.

The discussion involves the use of nine examples as clause types, and these may be listed here for convenience, with the numbering which they retain throughout the discussion:

    (i) *The barber shaved ten customers*
    (ii) *Ten customers were shaved*
    (iii) *The soldiers marched*
    (iv) *Mary seemed happy*
    (v) *The sergeant marched the soldiers*
    (vi) *The soldiers were marched*
    (vii) *The barber shaved* (sc. 'himself')
    (viii) *The barber shaved* (sc. 'customers')
    (ix) *The customers shaved* ('easily')

The discussion is broken into five sections for ease of presentation. Section 1 concerns the primary distinctions, and involves clauses (i) to (iv); section 2 concerns more delicate distinctions, and involves also clauses (v) to (vii); section 3 concerns the remaining two distinctions, and involves clauses (viii) and (ix). Section 4 presents a summary and discussion of the system network, and section 5 presents a brief discussion of verb classification in relation to transitivity systems.

SECTION 1

Presented with the clauses:

The barber shaved ten customers
Mary seemed happy

native speakers of English will agree that a 'passive transform' is possible with the first, but not with the second. That is,

The barber shaved ten customers———→*Ten customers were shaved*
(by the barber)

but not

Mary seemed happy———→*Happy was seemed (*by Mary*)

This is a long recognised and accepted feature of English grammar, and is included in even elementary grammar books. But it is important to say that surface grammar alone will not account for this relationship between

(i) *The barber shaved ten customers*

and

(ii) *Ten customers were shaved.*

Surface grammar will describe (i) differently from (ii), i.e. as SPC and SP(A) respectively. So sentences which native speakers feel are closely related will be shown as different, and sentences which are not felt to be closely related will be shown alike, since (i) will be analysed in a way similar to

(iv) *Mary seemed happy.*

At this stage we might postulate two clause types, and call them extensive and intensive; thus:

Transitivity————————→ ⎡Extensive (i, ii)
⎣Intensive (iv)

This is only giving names to well-known English clause types. We might then look to see if this distinction is characterised by any overt marking in surface structure. It may be that s is differently inflected in the types—since it may be suspected that different types of s are involved, one which can also occur (optionally) in an A (we may call this 'actor'), and one not so (we may call this 'attribuant'). The s is not so inflected in English; we can have:

He shaved the customers
He seemed nice

in which the element s is the same in surface structure. In some languages there would be an inflexional ending on the s in the extensive, marking it as the realisation of 'actor'.

We might consider a marking on the c; perhaps they are different types of c, and are marked as such. In (i) above the c is a noun-headed nominal group; in (iv) *Mary seemed happy* it is an adjective-headed nominal group. This, then, may be the distinction. In fact, this is a partial indication; an adjective-headed nominal group at c will mark a clause as intensive, because adjective-headed groups cannot operate at s (therefore no 'passive transform' is possible). But it is not the case that this will characterise all intensive clauses, because noun-headed groups can occur at c in intensive clauses. Thus:

Mary seemed a beautiful girl
He became a great painter.

We might, finally, consider the P in the clause types. Initially this would seem the most promising procedure. In the examples above *shave* and *seem* are different lexical verbs, and many native speakers want to account for the difference of clause types as 'lexical' differences in verbs and nothing more. If we consider further clauses such as

He eats fish (extensive)
She turned pale (intensive)

we will get similar results. It seems, therefore, that different lexical verbs characterise extensive and intensive clauses; and if we compile lists of which verbs occur in which types of clause this will give identifying criteria. Thus:

Extensive	*Intensive*
shave	seem
eat	turn
shoot	become.

But besides *She turned pale* (which will not transform → *Pale was turned) we find *She turned a page* (which will transform → A page was turned). And similarly:

He got cold	*He felt very fit*	*She turned out a good girl*
He got a present	*He felt the stone*	*She turned out good work.*

It is evident that the lexical verb alone will not identify all clauses as extensive or intensive. There is, in fact, no single criterion by which the distinction is marked. This is similar to what was said previously about the 'singular/plural' distinction (p. 19)—that there is no single identifying criterion for the feature 'plural'.

When we posit related features in a language, such as 'singular/plural', 'extensive/intensive', we are making a hypothesis (which is independent of the surface realisation of such features); this hypothesis must be tested as extensively as possible and, if validated, be formulated into an explicit statement. Thus, at word-rank we establish paradigms of nouns and so on, and this is a statement that the various forms in the paradigms are related to each other (whatever the difference in surface structure). What is being suggested here is that there are paradigms of clauses also, from which a selection of a particular form will be made in any instance. What follows may be viewed as an attempt to build up clause paradigms.

The element c is obligatory in intensive clauses, and so these differ from a clause such as (iii) *The soldiers marched* which has no c. So (iii) would seem to be extensive and (iv) *Mary seemed happy* is intensive. Thus:

$$\text{Transitivity} \longrightarrow \begin{cases} \text{Extensive (i), (ii), (iii)} \\ \text{Intensive (iv)} \end{cases}$$

The difference between the extensive clauses (i) and (iii) is that in (i) there is an *active* P with a following c, but (iii) has an *active* P with no following c. In semantic terms, the process in (i) is involved with two participants, an 'actor' (s) and a 'goal' (c); in (iii) there is only one participant, the 'actor', concerned in the process. In (ii) there are still (optionally) two participants involved, the 'goal' (now s, but still, of course, 'goal') and in a final (optional) adjunct, the 'actor', (now in the A, but still, of course, 'actor'). So (i) and (ii) need to be distinguished from (iii). These different types are called effective and descriptive. Thus:

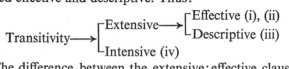

$$\text{Transitivity} \longrightarrow \begin{cases} \text{Extensive} \longrightarrow \begin{cases} \text{Effective (i), (ii)} \\ \text{Descriptive (iii)} \end{cases} \\ \text{Intensive (iv)} \end{cases}$$

The difference between the extensive: effective clauses (i) and (ii) is that (i) has an active P and a following c, but (ii) has a passive P and optionally a following A, and has at s what was the c in (i). In semantic terms, clause (i) has s as 'actor' and c as 'goal'; clause (ii) has s as 'goal' and optional A as 'actor'. These clause types are called operative and receptive respectively. Thus:

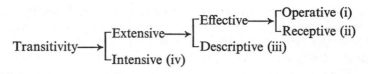

If the distinctions proposed and outlined in the final diagram are applied to the four example clauses, then each clause will have a different systemic description, though they will not each have a different structural description.

Example	Structure	Systemic description
(i) *The barber shaved ten customers*	SPC	extensive: effective: operative
(ii) *Ten customers were shaved*	SP	extensive: effective: receptive
(iii) *The soldiers marched*	SP	extensive: descriptive
(iv) *Mary seemed happy*	SPC	intensive

Such a systemic description will not only show similar surface structures to be realisations of different clause types, as (i) and (iv), but will also show the relative relationship of clauses of different or similar surface structure; so the fact that (i) and (ii) share two systemic features and differ only in a third suggests they are more closely related to each other than either is to (iii), which shares only one feature with each of them; but all three are contrasted with (iv), which shares no features with any of them.

SECTION 2

Indeed, if the clause types discussed in section 1 were the only clause types in English, then the above description would serve to identify each type uniquely. But we also find clauses such as:

(v) The sergeant marched the soldiers
(vi) The soldiers were marched.

In surface structure, these resemble clauses (i) and (ii), and are transforms of each other. They can obviously be labelled operative and receptive:

Operative	Receptive
(i) *The barber shaved ten customers*	(ii) *Ten customers were shaved*
(v) *The sergeant marched the soldiers*	(vi) *The prisoners were marched*

There are, however, distinctions which show that while (i) and (ii) are effective clauses as discussed above, (v) and (vi) are descriptive clauses, and are related to (iii) *The soldiers marched*.

Effective:operative clauses, such as (i), occur without an overt C element, but are interpreted in just the same way as when the C element is present. That is, clauses such as:

That barber shaves well

Mother washes on a Monday

occur regularly and are interpreted as meaning:

That barber shaves (people) well

Mother washes (the clothes) on a Monday

But clauses such as:

The sergeant marched

He sank

are not interpreted as meaning:

The sergeant marched the soldiers

He sank the boat

Semantically, native speakers agree that in the clause:

(i) *The barber shaved ten customers*

it is *the barber* who does the *shaving*; but in the clause:

(v) *The sergeant marched the soldiers*

it is *the soldiers* who do the *marching* (whether the *sergeant* does so or not—the clause does not specify this). In other words, the actor is realised as S in (i) but as C in (v). It is then evident that *the sergeant* (i.e. the S) in (v) is fulfilling a different role, is realising a different feature, from that in any of the other clauses. It is neither actor nor goal: this feature is called initiator (or causer, reflecting the fact that the combination of features (extensive):descriptive:operative is one way of expressing 'causation' in English). It would appear, therefore, that there are three possible participant roles which can be fulfilled by S in descriptive clauses. Thus:

(v) *The sergeant marched the soldiers*→S as initiator
  (descriptive:operative)

(vi) *The soldiers were marched*———→S as actor
  (descriptive:receptive)

(iii) *The soldiers marched*———————→S as initiator/actor (i.e.
  (descriptive:middle, the term   combines the roles)
  'middle' is used to distinguish
  from operative and receptive).

Effective clauses, on the other hand, have:

(i)   *The barber shaved ten customers*——→S as actor
    (effective: operative)

(ii) *Ten customers were shaved* ————→S as goal
    (effective: receptive).

The obvious question is whether there is a type of effective clause which combines the roles of actor and goal in a middle form, as the descriptive combines the roles of actor and initiator in a middle form. In English we have clauses such as:

The barber shaved himself/*He shaved himself*

where the reflexive complement (c^{Ref}) is treated as an extensive complement in clause structure: the reflexive does not take the tonic syllable in such clauses since it is a grammatical, not a lexical, item; it thus differs from the 'emphatic' reflexive as in *She asked the question herself* (*cf. She asked herself the question*). We also find clauses such as:

He shaved

He washed and dressed

which are interpreted as meaning:

He shaved himself

He washed and dressed himself

so that in:

(vii) *He shaved*

we have a combination of actor and goal in an effective: middle clause.

We can summarise the discussion thus far by saying that effective and descriptive are different types of extensive clauses; both of these types have an operative, a middle and a receptive form. Clauses which are:

effective: operative will have   S as actor, C as goal

effective: middle will have   S as actor and goal combined

effective: receptive will have   S as goal and A as actor (optionally)

descriptive: operative will have S as initiator and C as actor ('causative')

descriptive: middle will have   S as initiator and actor combined

descriptive: receptive will have S as actor and A as initiator (optionally).

Diagrammatically:

	Operative	*Middle*	*Receptive*
Effective	(i)	(vii)	(ii)
Descriptive	(v)	(iii)	(vi)

And the system network may now be represented as:

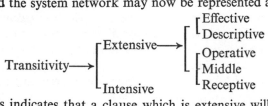

This indicates that a clause which is extensive will choose between effective and descriptive, and simultaneously between operative, middle and receptive.

SECTION 3

There are only two further distinctions to be taken into account. The first of these has already been mentioned. Clauses such as:

> He shaved
> Mother washes (on a Monday)

will be interpreted as meaning:

> He shaved himself
> Mother washes the things (on a Monday).

This means that the clause:

> (viii) The barber shaves (well)

is extensive: effective and is operative, since it has s as actor. The only difference between this clause and (i) is that in (i) we have a surface realisation of goal (at c), but in (viii) we do not. This can be simply represented as a choice between goal realised/goal unrealised. Thus:

$$(\text{Extensive:effective:operative})\longrightarrow\begin{cases}\text{Goal realised}\\\text{Goal unrealised.}\end{cases}$$

This choice presumes the prior selection of effective and operative: it is not open to descriptive: operative, since the c in such clauses is the actor; nor is it available to receptive clauses, since in such clauses the s is the goal.

The final clause type involves clauses such as (ix) *He shaves easily* meaning 'it is easy to shave him': such clauses are very common in present tense, and in certain contexts. Thus:

> They wash easily
> These books sell well
> This material wears well

In clause (ix) the relationship between 'the customer' (*he*) and *shaves* is as in the other clauses. That is, 'the customer' is still the goal. So we have an effective clause which is also receptive since it has s as goal, and so has the same features as (ii) *The customers were shaved*. There is an obvious surface difference between these clauses in that (ii) has a passive verbal group at P, but (ix) has an active verbal group at P. The (ii) type seems directed towards an actor, as is emphasised by the optional inclusion of actor at A:

> *The customers were shaved by the barber*

and the related interrogative clause is:

> (*the customers were shaved*)⟶*By whom? (Were they?)*

The type exemplified by (ix), on the other hand, seems directed towards the possibility or facility of the process, as is shown by the almost obligatory manner adverb:

> *This coat buttons easily*
>
> *This poem recites beautifully*

and the related interrogative clause:

> (*this coat buttons easily*)⟶*Does it?*

This distinction has been given the appropriate names of agent-oriented (ii), and process-oriented (ix). Thus:

$$(\text{Extensive:effective:receptive}) \longrightarrow \begin{bmatrix} \text{Agent-oriented} \\ \text{Process-oriented} \end{bmatrix}$$

This choice is obviously only open to effective:receptive clauses.

SECTION 4

Thus, with a total of nine clause types, we can represent the whole network as in Figure 11.

FIGURE 11

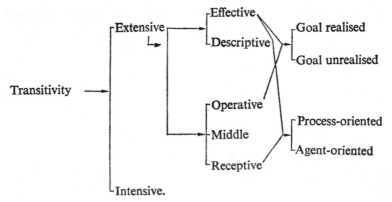

And the description of the clauses will be:

    (i) *The barber shaved ten customers*   SPC
        extensive: effective/operative: goal realised

   (ii) *Ten customers were shaved*   SP
        extensive: effective/receptive: agent-oriented

  (iii) *The soldiers marched*   SP
        extensive: descriptive: middle

  (iv) *Mary seemed happy*   SPC
        intensive

   (v) *The sergeant marched the soldiers*   SPC
        extensive: descriptive: operative

  (vi) *The soldiers were marched*   SP
        extensive: descriptive: receptive

 (vii) *The barber shaved* (sc. 'himself')   SP
        extensive: effective: middle

(viii) *The barber shaved* ('people')   SP
        extensive: effective: operative: goal unrealised

  (ix) *The customers shaved* ('easily')   SP
        extensive: effective: receptive: process-oriented.

In the above descriptions, some of the clauses have the same structural description (three have SPC, six have SP) but each has a unique systemic description. This means that if we consider structure as the way in which systemic features are realised we can assign unambiguous descriptions to each clause, but this is not so with structural description alone. We can, in other words, predict structure from system, but not system from structure: given the structural description SPC, it may be any one of three clause types above, and the structural description SP may represent any one of six clauses above; but given the feature specification

    extensive: descriptive: operative

we can predict the structure SPC, and we can further say that it will be a 'causative' clause, with s as initiator and c as actor. From the hearer's position, of course, ambiguity is obviously possible since it is structure he has to interpret. Halliday has pointed out that:

    Children don't wash easily

may be interpreted as any of the following:

  (vii) *Children find it difficult to wash themselves*
 (viii) *Children find it difficult to wash things*
  (ix) *It is difficult to wash children.*

Much of the foregoing discussion has been informal and semantic. We may note some more formal indications of the distinctions.

The distinction between extensive and intensive is fairly clear: an intensive clause must have an active P and must have a c^I present, and the verbs which can occur in such clauses form a fairly well defined class (though it must be remembered that some will also enter into other classes), traditionally called 'copula' class, e.g. *be, seem, turn, become, grow, appear, turn out, look, get*. Thus:

⌈Intensive——→verb of 'copula' class; active P; c^I present

⌊Extensive——→verb not of 'copula' class; c^E may be present

An operative clause will have an active verbal group at P; if it is a descriptive clause then a c^E will be present and the clause is 'causative'; if it is an effective clause then it may have a c^E present (goal realised) or it may not (goal unrealised).

A middle clause will have an active P whether it is effective or descriptive; but will have only one nominal element, namely s.

A receptive clause will have a passive P if it is descriptive; if it is effective it may have a passive P (agent-oriented) or it may have an active P (process-oriented).

The indication of distinctions within extensive clauses depends, however, on the distinction between effective and descriptive. This is the primary distinction within effective clauses, and it is this distinction which seems to present the essential difficulty of the transitivity systems.

The clause paradigms listed underneath are intended to illustrate the difference, and indeed to illustrate again what is meant by paradigmatic axis: given a feature such as 'effective' there is a choice from a list of possible clause types; given a feature like 'descriptive' there is a choice from a different list of possible clause types. It is the different possibilities of choice which enables us to posit features like effective and descriptive in the first place, not the other way round.

Effective	Descriptive
The barber shaved ten customers	*The soldiers marched*
Ten customers were shaved	*The sergeant marched them*
He shaved (sc. 'himself')	*The soldiers were marched*
The barber shaved ('well')	
The customer shaved ('easily')	
He sells books	*Corn grows*

Effective	Descriptive
Books are sold	*The farmer grows corn*
He sells (sc. 'himself'):	*Corn is grown*
non-occurring?	
He sells (sc. 'things')	
These books sell ('well')	
Mary washed the dishes	*The boat sank*
The dishes were washed	*He sank the boat*
Mary washed (sc. 'herself')	*The boat was sunk*
Mary washed (sc. 'the dishes')	
It washes ('easily')	

There are three points to note in relation to these paradigms:

(i) The occurrence of types (viii) and (ix) in the effective paradigm, as against the non-occurrence of such types in the descriptive paradigm. We can have in English:

> *she washes the clothes* or *she washes*
> *she dressed herself* or *she dressed*

where the alternatives are interpreted alike; but not

> *he sank the boat* or *he sank*
> *he grows corn* or *he grows*

without a difference in meaning.

(ii) In the effective paradigm, the operative clause may have either a c^E or a c^{Ref}, thus:

> *He kicked the ball: He kicked himself*
> *He washed the dishes: He washed himself.*

This is not so with the operative in the descriptive paradigm, thus:

> *He marched the soldiers: *He marched himself*
> *He sank the boat: *He sank himself.*

The fact that c^{Ref} can occur in descriptive: operative clauses with certain accompanying adverbial elements of clause structure:

> *He marched himself down the road*
> *He sank himself into the nearest chair*

does not invalidate the important point that in effective: operative clauses the c^{Ref} can occur without such adverbials, but this is not so in descriptive clauses.

(iii) If clauses with double complements are considered (pp. 57 *ff.*) it becomes evident that not all clause types will accept two complements. The first complement in the clause:

He gave John a present

is usually called 'indirect object': it must precede the other c, and it may be realised as a 'to/for' adjunct, as in:

He gave a present to John

This is sometimes referred to as 'dative case'; but the fact that the element in question can also occur as s:

John was given a present

(where 'dative' is surely inappropriate) argues against this. The important point is that *John* realises the same feature in all three clause positions. This feature has been called 'beneficiary' (i.e. one who or that which benefits from the process of the clause—for good or ill). Only effective clauses can accept a beneficiary. Thus:

He gave John a book	**He marched John the soldiers*
A book was given John but not	**The soldiers were marched John*
John was given a book	**John was marched the soldiers*

SECTION 5

It is obviously possible to classify verbs according to their occurrence in the effective or descriptive (or intensive) paradigm. This should yield a more satisfactory classification than the traditional 'transitive/intransitive' classification; and we will not have to talk about 'intransitive verb used transitively' in:

Boys fly kites
He sank the boat

or 'transitive verb used intransitively' in:

These books sell well
This cloth washes beautifully,

to say nothing of 'used reflexively, absolutely, absolutely (for refl.)'.

There will, indeed, still be some overlap; some verbs will enter into more than one class, which is why we said verb classes will not identify clause types, for example *grow* in:

He grew pale   ('copula')
He grew   ('descriptive')

but the overlap should be minimised.

Not all verbs will realise all possibilities of the paradigms; but it is difficult to say that any particular verb will not occur in any

FIGURE 12 *Systems at Clause Rank*

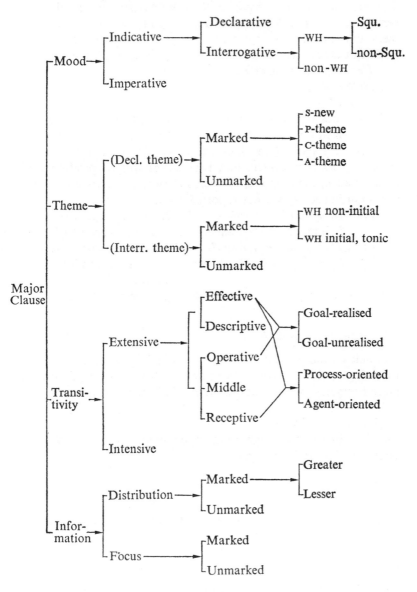

I

particular clause type. Given a suitable context, it seems that any of the possibilities of the paradigm will be generated by the grammar. The most obvious is type (vii) in the effective paradigm; only a few verbs—*wash, shave, dress*—occur regularly in such clauses. It might seem more appropriate, therefore, to consider this as a subclass of (viii). But other verbs do occur, if less regularly or frequently:

> *He flung out of the office*
> *Hold still*
> *Behave!*

This indicates that it is a genuine clause type, and new examples can be formed on the model if desired. Other verbs will only occur in types (viii) and (ix) in highly restricted circumstances: but such circumstances may obtain, and the clauses will be produced. We might predict, for example, the verbs *demand* and *encourage* would not occur in such types, but reported examples are:

> (viii) *He demands all the time*   (He demands (things) all the time)
> *I do that because it encourages*   (Encourages people)
> (ix) *They encourage too easily*   (It is too easy to encourage them)
> *They don't demand any more*   (Nobody demands them any more)

A chart of all systems at clause rank is given in Figure 12.

3.2   Systems at Group Rank

The unit Group provides the environment for further systems. The following sections provide a first approach to a description of the more prominent systems at Nominal and Verbal Group.

3.2.1   Nominal Group

The principal systems operating at Nominal Group are those of Number, Case and Gender.

3.2.1.1   NUMBER

The system of number is usually regarded as a feature of word-rank, and as a system having the terms singular and plural. That is:

$$\text{Number} \longrightarrow \begin{bmatrix} \text{Singular} \\ \text{Plural} \end{bmatrix}$$

It is true that the terms in the number system are to a large extent realised morphologically at word-rank; thus we can say:

> *boy* = singular: *boys* = plural.

As discussed earlier, however, not all nouns are overtly marked for number, and those that are can be marked in different ways. There is not one invariable criterion by which the terms singular and plural are marked. Rather, there are a number of criteria, one or more of which may be present in any instance.

Also, it is not the case that only nouns realise terms in the number system. Words which operate at *d* and at *o* in the nominal group also choose for number. Thus:

Singular	Plural
that	*those*
one	*two* (etc.)

There are, therefore, nominal groups which contain a number realisation at *d* and/or at *o* but not at *h*, and which can be thus identified as singular or plural groups:

Singular	Plural
this sheep	*those sheep*
one sheep	*two sheep.*

Some items which occur at *d* do not select for number (*the, all, my,* etc.), and some items which occur at *o* do not select for number (ordinal numerals—*first, second, third,* etc.).

Two points emerge from such considerations. First, number would seem to be more appropriately assigned to group rank, since it can be realised at any one of three places in nominal group structure. Second, since all three places can be filled by words which do not choose for number, it is possible to have nominal groups which may be described as uncountable, as opposed to nominal groups which do choose for number, and which may be described as countable. The system of number would therefore be more properly represented as:

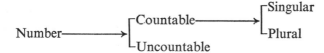

The terms in the system will be realised by certain items at *d*, at *o* and at *h*. Thus:

	at *d*	at *o*	at *h*
Singular:	*a, this, that, each, either, every*	*one*	any singular noun (i.e. any noun morphologically marked)
Plural:	*these, those, many, few*	*two, three* etc.	any plural noun (i.e. any noun morphologically marked)

Uncountable: *all, the, such, first, second*   any unmarked noun
                some, no, my etc.   (e.g. *sheep, deer*)

It is the number of the nominal group which determines agreement with the verbal group at P, and with pronominal groups in succeeding clauses. It is obvious that pronouns also realise terms in the number system. Thus:

When the boys come, they will tell us

When the boy comes, he will tell us

A singular nominal group exhibits agreement with P in that the -s form of the verb will occur where appropriate (i.e. in present tense, third person). A plural nominal group in the same environment will not be followed by the -s form of the verb. An uncountable nominal group in such an environment will have either the -s form or not the -s form following. Thus:

    Singular: *The bird sings   This sheep walks*
    Plural: *The birds sing   Those sheep walk*
    Uncountable: *The sheep grazes   The sheep graze.*

We can, of course, identify each occurrence of *the sheep was/were* as singular or plural by the agreement exhibited with the following verb (or pronominal group), and we can rightly consider such agreement to be a realisation of a term in the number system. There are two points to note, however: (i) we are not identifying with reference only to the nominal group in question, but with reference to a relation between the nominal group and another verbal group (or pronominal group); and (ii) we can make no generalised statement, and grammar is concerned with generalised statements, not with citation of particular items: the generalised statement for the nominal group in this case is that it is unmarked for number.

From the previous discussion of inflexions in nouns, it is obvious that there are four main classes of nouns (which can be variously subclassified) according to their operation in singular, plural and unmarked nominal groups; and pronouns can obviously be classified according to number. In other words, although the system of number is here being assigned to group rank, it is not irrelevant to word rank, since words are overtly marked in their own structure for singular and plural, and, by default, unmarked. Thus:

NOUN

1. Either sg. or pl.	2. Always sg.	3. Always pl.	4. Unmarked
boy	beauty	clergy	sheep
lad	courage	people	deer
bat	despair	dregs	fish
horse	mathematics	bellows	fowl
etc.	etc.	etc.	etc.

PRONOUN

1. sg.	2. pl.	3. Unmarked
I/me	we/us	mine/our
he/him	they/them	you/your
she/her		his/its
it		her/their

In terms of this classification there is a difficulty in assigning the traditional 'collective' nouns to classes (e.g. *army, committee*). Such nouns are regular members of class 1 according to their own structure, since they morphologically distinguish singular and plural forms. They are irregular in that their singular form occurs in nominal groups which take a following -s form of the verb or not an -s form of the verb, e.g.

The committee was/were . . .

Semantically, of course, this is a reflection of the referents of the words being thought of as a corporate body (singular) or a collection of individuals (plural); it may also relate to different varieties of English, different 'styles'.

3.2.1.2 CASE

The system of case in English nouns has two terms, a marked and an unmarked term. The unmarked term is usually called the common case and the marked term the possessive or genitive case. For the marked case neither of the names is really suitable; the function of the case is to mark relation certainly, but this relation may be one of a number of types of relation, and certainly not only one of possession. It would perhaps be better to use terms such as marked/ unmarked, but the names common and genitive are reasonably neutral and are well established (though 'possessive' is inappropriate). Thus:

		Genitive
Singular	Common	
	boy	*boy's*
	horse	*horse's*
	man	*man's*
	men	*men's*
Plural	*boys*	*boys'*
	daughters	*daughters'*

Perhaps the only real problem of case in English is whether it is a feature of word rank or of group rank (or has relevance for both, as the number system). We usually think of case as applicable to nouns, and certainly nouns form paradigms according to realisation of case and number features:

> *boy   boys   ox   oxen*
> *boy's   boys'   ox's   oxen's.*

When the noun operates at *d* in nominal group structure it is the genitive form which occurs:

> *the boy's book/the boys' book*
> *the ox's tail/the oxen's tails.*

It is clear, however, that the *'s* is in fact added to a complete nominal group. That this is so is evidenced by the fact that nominal groups containing qualifiers can operate at *d* (and are therefore rank-shifted) in this way, and when they are the *'s* occurs after the qualifier, not after the headword. Thus:

> *the [shop across the road]'s sales have gone up.*

Further, it is possible in English to transform a qualifier with the structure 'of + nominal group' into a *d* element, which is marked by the *'s*. Thus:

> *The houses of the town council   The town council's houses.*

We lose one *the* in such a transform, since we do not say in English:

> * *The the town council's houses*

We might (quite arbitrarily) consider it to be the second *the* which has been excised, and thus the analysis is:

> *The [town council]'s houses.*

The problem with such an analysis is that it seems to treat *'s* as a word, since it is operating in group structure, or alternatively to treat *town council* as a word taking an enclitic *'s* morpheme. The choice would seem to be between downgrading *town council* from group to word, or upgrading *'s* from morpheme to word. Neither solution is satisfactory, since *'s* is unlike any item we want to call a word, and *(the) town council* is clearly a group and not a word.

There is perhaps another possibility, if we consider more carefully the concept of rankshift. A unit does not become another unit when it is rankshifted, but operates at an element of structure usually realised by a lower unit. A rankshifted unit therefore retains its own structure but can realise features usually realised by a unit of lower rank. Thus, the feature 'actor' is usually realised by a nominal group at s; but if a clause is rankshifted to s then it can realise this feature. Thus:

> s = Actor
> ⟦*Whoever comes last*⟧ *will kill him*

just as

> s = Actor
> *John will kill him.*

Similarly the group *(the) town council* is rankshifted to operate at *d* in another group; it retains its own structure, but realises features of 'specification' (see p. 128) usually realised by a word. The *'s* can be regarded as an overt marker of this rankshift and feature realisation only, and its structural value need not be stated. This is perhaps but another unsatisfactory solution, though it has resemblances to similar problems elsewhere in the grammar, notably the linker *and* and intonation features which are regarded as realisations of systemic terms, but are not considered as constituents of structure.

3.2.1.3 GENDER

Gender is usually said to be 'natural' in English. This means that the contextually-determined classes of masculine, feminine and neuter are reflected by the grammatical system of gender; in other words, nouns referring to males are masculine in gender, nouns referring to females are feminine in gender and nouns referring to neither are neuter in gender. This is largely, but by no means completely, true for English. The formal indication of gender in English is agreement between nominal groups and the gender-bearing pronouns *he, she, it*. (The only remnant of morphemic indication of gender which need be noticed is the derivational -ess, which marks feminine gender in nouns such as *authoress, actress*. Even this word-structure marker has decreased greatly in use in recent times, and periphrases such as *male-teacher, woman doctor* are now common.)

It follows from what was said above that if gender were completely natural in English there would be three gender classes, as follows:

Masculine, correlating with the pronoun *he*
Feminine, correlating with the pronoun *she*
Neuter, correlating with the pronoun *it*.

There are, indeed, many nouns (or rather, noun-headed groups, since it is the whole group for which the pronoun can substitute; this is why I have incorporated gender into the group systems, though it is obviously relevant at word rank also) which do fulfil this correlation, e.g.:

Masculine: *man, uncle, grandfather, actor, boy, bachelor, William, son*; *Time, Death*
Feminine: *woman, aunt, girl, actress, mother, daughter, maid, Avril*; *Nature, Charity*
Neuter: *wood, can, tin, tree, holiday, Sunday, bible, force, abstraction, fission*

It should be noted that the gender of these items is not, in fact, determined by the sex of the referent. It is sometimes said that we need to know the meaning of the noun in order to know its gender. This is not necessary, and in any case would fail with personifications such as *Death, Charity*; all that needs to be known is the pronominal correlation, e.g.

Death, man   *he*
Charity, girl   *she*
box, mountain   *it*

There are many other nouns, however, which do not stand in a one-to-one correlation with pronouns. The correlations which they exhibit are various, and they can be subclassified on this basis:

(i) Nouns which correlate with either *he* or *she*. These are largely nouns denoting occupations, human relationships and some proper names, e.g.

doctor, teacher, pupil, companion, servant, boss, supervisor, Terry, person

Such nouns are usually said to have common gender. It is true in this class that gender determination in any occurring instance is determined by sex of the referent. Agreement with *he* or *she* is in accordance with the known or assumed sex of the referent; in a number of cases there is a bias towards a particular correlation where the referent is not known, thus *doctor* more frequently collocates with *he*, and *teacher* with *she*.

(ii) Nouns which correlate with either *he* or *it*; mainly animate, non-human nouns such as:

insect, spider, beetle, cock, ram, bull

(iii) Nouns which correlate with *she* or *it*; these include animate, non-human nouns, nouns referring to machines or engines, and place names, such as:

mare, ewe; ship, car, train; country, Britain

(iv) Nouns correlating with *he* or *she* or *it*, mainly names of animals and non-adult humans, such as:

deer, dog, cat, horse, cow; baby, child, tot

In none of the groups (ii), (iii) or (iv) is sex the determining factor for occurring correlations (or obviously for many of them there would not be alternatives). The type of language and speaker, the register, seem to be the relevant factors.

We can perhaps bring together all the subclasses as unmarked for gender, and they can be further specified if desired. Thus:

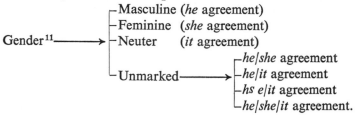

Systems at group rank are summarised in Figure 13.

FIGURE 13   *Systems at (Nominal) Group Rank*

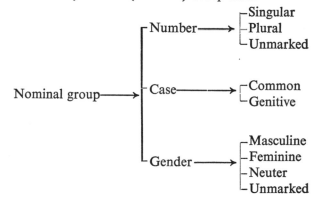

3.2.2   *Systems at* d *in Nominal Group Structure*

The general word-class which realises the element d in nominal group structure is called determiner. Determiners may obviously be subclassified according to their operation in the substructures $d_1d_2d_3$ (pp. 30-31). Determiners may also be subclassified along various dimensions according to their realisation of systemic terms.

Perhaps the primary function of determiners is, as the name suggests, to determine or identify. They identify the class which the headword expounds, and may or may not specify a particular member of that class. Some determiners are therefore specific and some are non-specific. Thus, in the nominal groups *a house, any house*, the determiners do not specify any particular *house*. But in the groups *my house, this house*, the determiners specify that it is 'that member of the class "house" which belongs to me' and 'that member of the class "house" which is nearer us' that are being referred to. We can therefore consider specification to be the primary system here, with the terms specific and non-specific. Thus:

$$\text{Specification} \rightarrow \begin{bmatrix} \text{Specific}\,(the, my, your, John's, which, whose, \text{etc.}) \\ \text{Non-specific}\,(a, any, all, both, neither, \text{etc.}) \end{bmatrix}$$

The specific determiners may specify by various means, or they may not specify in themselves but merely indicate that specification will be given. There is a system of selection with the terms selective or non-selective from which specific determiners choose. The only specific:non-selective determiner in English is *the*: what in fact this item does in the language is to indicate that something in the cotext (the surrounding language) or in the context (the situation of the utterance) will identify the member in question of the class denoted by the headword. Thus, in the groups

(throw) *the ball*

(hit) *the thing*

the identification is likely to be situational: only one *ball* or *thing* will be present (or perhaps pointed to); in the groups

the university of Glasgow

the man who came to dinner

the determiner points forward to the qualifier in the groups which identifies the member of the class *university* and the class *man*. All other specific determiners are selective; they select from the various means of identification. Thus:

$$\text{(Specific) selection} \longrightarrow \begin{bmatrix} \text{Selective}\,(this, my, your, mother's, \text{etc.}) \\ \text{Non-selective}\,(the). \end{bmatrix}$$

Determiners which are specific:selective may select a means of identification from the possibilities available. The selection may be according to a genitival relation or a non-genitival relation; the first of these features is obviously realised by the genitive form of pronouns and by rankshifted nominal groups as discussed in the previous section. We can call this system selectivity, meaning that it is the selection of the means of identification of the member of the class denoted by the headword. Thus:

(Specific, selective) ⟶ ⎡Genitival (*my, your, John's*, etc.)
selectivity   ⎣Non-genitival (*this, that, which*, etc.)

The determiners which are genitival will make a further choice between nominal, pronominal and relative; and genitival:pronominal determiners will make further selection from the system of person. Thus:

Specific ⎫   ⎡Nominal (*John's, mother's*, etc.)
Selective ⎬relation^1⟶ ⎢Pronominal→person→ ⎡1st (*my*)
Genitival ⎭   ⎢   ⎨2nd (*your*)
                                ⎣Relative (*whose*)   ⎣3rd (*his, her, its*)

The determiners which are non-genitival are also involved in a further system, which we may call relation^2, according to whether they are relative or demonstrative. Thus:

Specific ⎫   ⎡Relative (*which, what*)
Selective ⎬relation^2 ⟶ ⎢
Non-genitival ⎭   ⎣Demonstrative (*this, that*)

Determiners which are non-specific according to the primary division set up indicate a class but do not specify any particular member of that class. They may, however, refer to the whole class or parts of the class; so we can say they choose from a system of coverage which has the terms total and partial. If total is selected, then the reference may be to all the members of the class or to none of the members, so we can say there is a system of clusion with the terms inclusive and exclusive. Thus:

                                   ⎡Inclusive (*all, every, each, both*)
        ⎡Total→clusion→ ⎢
Coverage→ ⎢   ⎣Exclusive (*no, neither*)
        ⎣Partial (*a, some, any, another, either*)

This is not the only way in which determiners may be classified. It may seem unnecessary to subclassify to such a degree, though further division is necessary if the items are to be uniquely classified. If items such as determiners are 'grammatical' rather than 'lexical' items then the grammar must uniquely specify them. Thus the feature description:

determiner: specific: selective: genitival: pronominal: 1st person

means (is realised by) only one item in the language, namely *my*.

It can be seen that further subclassification is possible, and all such items can be uniquely specified in this way. The items *no*, *neither*, for example, will—according to what has been considered so far—both be described as:

determiner: non-specific: total: exclusive

and the application of a choice between dual and non-dual (in a system of duality) will distinguish them. Thus:

no   determiner: non-specific: total: exclusive: non-dual
neither   determiner: non-specific: total: exclusive: dual.

Systems at deictic in nominal group structure are summarised in Figure 14.

FIGURE 14   *Systems at deictic in Nominal Group Structure*

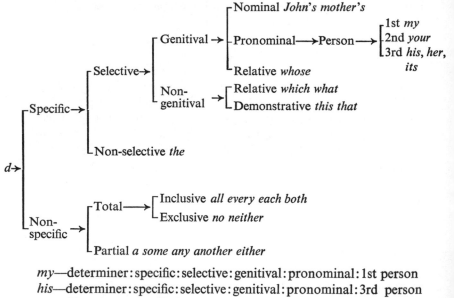

my—determiner: specific: selective: genitival: pronominal: 1st person
his—determiner: specific: selective: genitival: pronominal: 3rd person
   (singular: masculine).

3.2.3 *Verbal Group*

It was stated above (p. 41) that the verbal group is one of the most complex areas of English grammar. This is so because the verbal group is the environment for a number of systemic choices and the terms selected are not in a one-to-one relation with their realisation in structure. There are at least eight systems relevant to the verbal group; but not all verbal groups can choose from all systems (only finite groups can choose from all systems); and it is also the case that most of the systems are binary and non-recursive. That is, we choose one from two possible terms, and we make the choice only once in a group. The main complexity, in fact, is occasioned by the tense system, which is not binary and which is recursive. The principal systems are:

1. Finiteness
2. Modality
3. Tense
4. Polarity
5. Aspect
6. Voice
7. Contrast
8. Focus (of Contrast).

3.2.3.1 FINITENESS

As already discussed, the system of finiteness is a primary distinction in the verbal group; further systemic choices depend on selection here, and the choice here is also relevant to clause classification since a finite verbal group is obligatory in an independent clause and a non-finite verbal group is one criterion of a dependent clause. The system has the terms finite and non-finite, thus:

$$\text{Finiteness} \longrightarrow \begin{cases} \text{Finite} \\ \text{Non-finite} \end{cases}$$

and realisation of the selected term occurs at initial position in the verbal group. As shown in the diagram on p. 44, the terms and realisations are:

System	Terms	Realisation (*at initial element*)
Finiteness	Finite	-s, -d, base form of the verb, or modal
	Non-finite	-ing, -en, t-inf., base, form of the verb.

3.2.3.2 MODALITY

Since modal verbs are always finite it is evident that only finite verbal groups will select for modality; and further, since finiteness is realised at initial element in group structure, then if a modal verb is present it will be the initial element. There is, in practice, no need to mark a verbal group finite:modal since the marking modal will presume marking finite. The choice in the system of modality is a choice between a marked and an unmarked term, the presence of an element contrasting with its absence, and can therefore be named modal and non-modal. Thus:

System	*Terms*	*Realisation (at initial element)*
Modality	Modal	any modal verb
	Mon-modal	any other group

3.2.3.3 TENSE [12]

Discussion of the system of tense in English tends to be complicated by three factors:

   (i) confusion of tense and aspect
   (ii) confusion of tense and time reference
   (iii) non-consideration of more complex tense formations.

Though there is obvious reason for the confusion between tense and aspect in English, it has been maintained that they are different systems (p. 44), and should be kept apart in description. Accordingly, names such as 'continuous present' 'past perfect' are not used in this discussion. The components 'continuous/perfect' refer to aspectual features, and their combination with tense features serves only to blur the tense features which are involved.

The confusion of tense with time reference stems largely from the conception that the tense system is a reflection of some 'naturally-given' time system. This in turn leads to the view that past/present/future time is necessarily expressed by past/present/future tense in language. Not only is such correspondence not necessary, but tense, in fact, need not be a feature of a language—though such a language may perfectly well refer to time. The point is that time reference can be made by devices other than tense, and in English is often made by adverbial groups rather than verbal groups. It is not denied that there is a close relation between tense and time reference in English; but before this relation is discussed an adequate description of tense itself is required. In what follows the discussion is limited to discussing tense as a system of the verbal group.

In any attempt to describe the formation of compound tenses in English it becomes obvious that the regularity of formation processes permits compound tenses which have a number of components. It is not enough to account for the tense in verbal groups such as:

will come
will be coming
will have come

because considerably more complex forms are found:

will have been coming
will have been going to be coming
has been going to have been coming

It is true that the more complex of the theoretical possibilities do not occur nearly as frequently as the less complex possibilities. In spoken English, however, longer verbal groups which involve complex tense features are by no means uncommon, notwithstanding the fact that most native speakers are quite unaware of this. It is perhaps because the participants in a spoken situation already know the temporal implications of the discourse (they do not have to 'work them out') that such complexity is tolerated more in the spoken than in the written language. Nevertheless, the important point is that if a particular context requires the formulation of a particular combination of tense features then the grammar of the language (within certain stateable restrictions) will generate the required tense complex.

This last point is one further illustration of the inadequacy of a grammar which will only describe a given corpus. A grammar should not only describe what has occurred, but should be capable of predicting what structures and combinations may occur.

Traditionally, the tense system in English has three terms: present, past, future. They are retained here without comment for the primary distinction. Thus:

The term present is realised by the -s, base forms of the verb (*I eat*; *he eats*); the term past is realised by the -d form of the verb (*he ate/walked*); the term future is realised by will/shall + base form of the verb (*I will eat*; *they shall eat*); the primary distinctions are thus:

$$\text{Tense} \longrightarrow \begin{cases} \text{Present} \longrightarrow \text{-s, base form of verb} \\ \text{Past} \longrightarrow \text{-d form of verb} \\ \text{Future} \longrightarrow \text{will/shall + base form of verb} \end{cases}$$

Complexity is occasioned by the fact that English permits compound tenses; in other words, tense is recursive—it may be chosen more than once in the verbal group. This fact in itself need not occasion complexity; recursion is a feature occurring at various points in the grammar, and can be described as a depth relation (counting from the 'head' element). Thus:

$$e_3 \quad e_2 \qquad e_1$$

adjectives at e in nominal group structure: *the funny old American hat*

$$f_1 \quad f_2$$

derivation (f) in word structure: *boy* + *ish* + *ness*

In these examples, however, the elements which are recursive are realised by discrete items; they can be marked off and numbered. In the realisation of compound tenses in the verbal group this is not so; when there is a second tense element in the verbal group, the first tense element does not remain as above but undergoes a change in form and requires two items for its realisation. If we have the simple tense present (e.g. *eats*) and we wish to add past, we do not say **was eats* but rather *was eating*. This means that if there is more than one tense element in a verbal group, the (simple) present will be realised by the -ing form of the verb preceded by some part of the verb *be*; if the (simple) tense is past then in a compound tense this requires the -en form of the verb preceded by some part of the verb *have* (*has/had eaten*); if the (simple) tense is future then in a compound tense this requires *going to* + base form of the verb preceded by some part of the verb *be*. It is more accurate, therefore, to give two realisations of the simple tenses. Thus:

	1 item verbal group	more than 1 item verbal group
Present	-s form	*be* + -ing form
Past	-d form	*have* + -en form
Future	*will* + base form	*be* + *going to* + base form

The particular form of *be* and *have* which occurs in such structures will realise the second component of the compound tense.

In a verbal group such as *is eating*, we have placed the present (*be* + -ing) in the present (*is*); but in the group *was eating*, we have placed the present (*be* + -ing) in the past (*was*); and in the group *will be eating*, we have placed the present (*be* + -ing) in the future (*will* + base). These compound tenses can then be read as present in present, present in past, present in future.

We can in similar fashion place the past in the three terms, and this requires *have* as the tense auxiliary. In the group *has eaten*, we have placed the past (*have* + -en) in the present (*has*); in the group *had eaten*, we have placed the past (*have*+-en) in the past (*had*); and in the group *will have eaten*, we have placed the past (*have* + -en) in the future (*will* + base). We can then read these compound tenses as past in present, past in past, past in future.

We can also place the future in the three other terms. In this case the compound tenses are realised by some part of the verb *be* + base. In the group *is going to eat*, we have placed the future (*be going to* + base) in the present (*is*); in the group *was going to eat*, we have placed the future (*be going to* + base) in the past (*was*); in the group *will be going to eat*, we have placed the future (*be going to* + base) in the future (*will* + base). These compound tenses can then be read as future in present, future in past, future in future.

In summary: a verbal group with only one element of structure realises one of the primary tenses present, past; a verbal group with the auxiliary *will/shall* + base form of the verb realises the primary tense future. Each tense can then be chosen a second time in combination with itself or either of the others; such compound tenses are not realised by discrete elements, but require that the (simple) present be realised by some part of the verb *be* + the -ing form of the verb, that the (simple) past be realised by some part of the verb *have* + -en form of the verb and that the (simple) future be realised by some part of the verb *be* + *going to* + base form of the verb. The second component of the compound tense will be realised by the particular form of the verb *be* or *have* in the structures.

We have, therefore, three simple tenses and nine compound tenses, giving a total of twelve structures at this point. Figure 15 illustrates how the tenses are built up and how they may be read.

This takes tense to two places in the verbal group (counting back from lexical verb). Since tense may go up to five places, it is evident that long verbal groups realising quite complex tense formations are possible. There are however some restrictions: each term can only follow itself once in a group; the term present can only further occur at final position; the term future can only occur twice in a group. It may be useful to extend Figure 15 to three places; because

K

FIGURE 15

	Present	Past	Future
Simple	*eats*	*ate*	*will eat*
Present in	*is eating*	*was eating*	*will be eating*
Past in	*has eaten*	*had eaten*	*will have eaten*
Future in	*is going to eat*	*was going to eat*	*will be going to eat*

of the restrictions just given this means only four additional structures, as shown in Figure 16.

In order to analyse the tense of a compound verbal group it is

FIGURE 16

	Present	Past	Future
Simple	*eats*	*ate*	*will eat*
Present in Past in Future in	*is eating* *has eaten* *is going to eat*	*was eating* *had eaten* *was going to eat*	*will be eating* *will have eaten* *will be going to eat*
Present in Past in Present in Future in	*has been eating* *is going to be eating*	*had been eating* *was going to be eating*	*will have been eating* *will be going to be eating*
Past in Future in	*is going to have eaten*	*was going to have eaten*	*will be going to have eaten*
Future in Past in	*has been going to eat*	*had been going to eat*	*will have been going to eat*

obviously necessary to consider pairs of items in the group. Counting
begins from the lexical verb and moves back. If the final verb is an
-ing form this will indicate present, if it is an -en form this will

indicate past and if it is a base form this will indicate future. Thus:

(*be*)-ing———————————→*present*
(*have*) -en———————————→*past*
(*be going to*) base————————→*future*

If the tense goes to three places the items preceding the lexical verb need to be considered as a pair, and then the third item singly, to give the third component of the tense. Reading back from the lexical verb, items one and two equal the first component of the compound tense, items two and three equal the second component of the compound tense, and item three equals the third component of the compound tense. Thus:

3.2.3.4   POLARITY

The system of polarity is a system with the terms positive and negative, and in this system there is a one-to-one correlation realisation, because the term negative is always realised by the negator (*not, n't*). So this system is simply:

System	Terms	*Realisation*
Polarity———→	⌐Positive ———→	any group without negator
	⌊Negative———→	*not, n't*

3.2.3.5   ASPECT

The system of aspect has been confused with that of tense, and in certain respects the two do merge. But they are different systems and should be kept apart in description. Aspect is perhaps best considered primarily as a distinction between imperfective and perfective. The difference between the clauses

(i) *I have eaten the apple*

(ii) *I am eating the apple*

is (apart from tense) that in (i) attention is drawn to the fact that the action is completed, but in (ii) attention is directed to the fact that the action is in progress, is continuing. The contrast is not, however, between complete/incomplete in reference to a non-linguistic event.

It is simply that the language directs attention in this way. In the clause

(iii) *I was eating the apple*

the action is complete since it is in past time, but attention is still drawn to the continuance over an unspecified period of time of the action. It is the tense, and only the tense which differs between (ii) and (iii). This is why we ought to distinguish between aspect and tense. The clauses

(i) *I have eaten the apple*

(ii) *I am eating the apple*

differ in tense, (i) being past in present, (ii) being present in present; and they differ in aspect, (i) being perfective, and (ii) being imperfective. But the clauses

(ii) *I am eating the apple*

(iii) *I was eating the apple*

differ only in tense, (i) being present in present, and (ii) being present in past; but both are imperfective aspect.

There are a number of problems involved in any comprehensive discussion of aspect in English, but a primary division such as is being suggested here may provide a starting point and may help to illustrate that aspect and tense are different systems. Thus:

System	*Terms*	*Realisation*
Aspect	⌈Perfective——→*have* + -en	
	⌊Imperfective—→*be* + -ing	

3.2.3.6 VOICE

The system of voice in English has two terms, active and passive, the former being unmarked and the latter realised by part of the verb *be* + -en form of the verb. The system is simply thus:

System	*Terms*	*Realisation*
Voice	⌈Active———→any group not marked as passive	
	⌊Passive———→(part of) *be* + -en.	

This system is obviously closely related to the transitivity systems, since the distinction between operative (*John washed the dishes*) and receptive (*The dishes were washed by John*) requires, among other things, an active verbal group at P in the former and a passive verbal group at P in the latter. But it was pointed out that the correlation was not one-to-one, because clauses such as

This poem recites well
This coat buttons easily
It shows to advantage here
are receptive clauses (they have s as goal), though they have active
verbal groups. It would, of course, be possible to talk about receptive/
active and receptive/passive clauses; but this would be combining
features of clause and group rank. It seems more appropriate to
assign the features operative and receptive to clause rank, and the
features active and passive to group rank.

Some verbs do not admit of a passive form (see intensive clauses,
pp. 107 *ff.*). There are no passive equivalents of
He resembled his brother
He had a great set of cards.

3.2.3.7 CONTRAST

The system here being called contrast is one of the possibilities of
marked tonicity (pp. 101 *ff.*). In the (clause final) verbal group
(John) has been *ask*ed
the tonic syllable falls on the lexical verb. The tonic may be moved to
another item in the verbal group, thus contrasting with the neutral
position. We can, therefore, distinguish a contrastive/non-contras-
tive opposition:

System	Terms	Realisation
Contrast⟶	┌Non-contrastive⟶	tonic on lexical verb
	└Contrastive⟶	tonic elsewhere in the group

3.2.3.8 FOCUS (OF CONTRAST)

If the verbal group is contrastive, one of three elements may provide the focus of contrast. If the verbal group contains a modal
verb it may be this item which provides the focus. Thus:
(He) *should* come
(He) *can* come
(He) *may* manage it.
If the verbal group is positive it may be the positive element which
provides the focus, and the fact that it is the positiveness of the
group which is being emphasised and not the lexicality of the item
at *l*, is shown in that the auxiliary *do* is required when the non-
contrastive form would be a verbal group with only an *l* element of

structure, and that we usually require the full form of an auxiliary, not the enclitic form. Thus:

Non-contrastive	Contrastive
He's *com*ing	He *is* coming
He *came*	He *did* come
He *comes*	He *does* come.

If the verbal group is negative in polarity then the negative element may provide the focus; this usually requires the full form of the negator and not the enclitic form. Thus:

Non-contrastive	Contrastive
He isn't *com*ing	He's *not* coming
He won't *do* it	He will *not* do it.

FIGURE 17 *Systems at Verbal Group Rank*

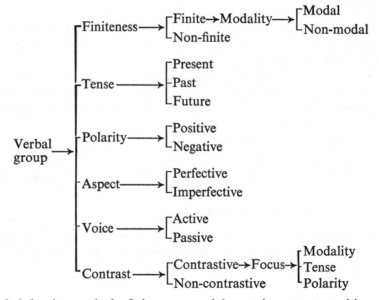

(John) *has* been asked—finite, non-modal, past in present, positive, perfective, passive, contrastive/polarity.

Finally, the focus of contrast may be provided by the tense element. Thus:

Non-contrastive	Contrastive
He's been *asked*	He's *been* asked.

We may, therefore, though this is simplifying somewhat, show the system as

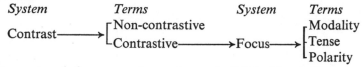

Systems at verbal group rank are shown in full in Figure 17.

Notes

1. Randolph Quirk: *The Use of English*, Longmans Green & Co.;
1962: pp. 176 *ff.*
2. Although the procedure of comparing word-pairs to identify
morphemic constituents of words is well established, the principle
of 'squares' is taken from J. H. Greenberg: 'The Definition of
Linguistic Units' in *Essays in Linguistics*, University of Chicago
Press; 1957.
3. Nominal group: parts of the presentation here derive from the
excellent presentation of nominal group structure given by J. M.
Sinclair: *A Course in Spoken English, Part 3: Grammar*, Oxford
University Press; 1965 (limited issue).
4. Verbal group: for more detailed and lucid description see F. R.
Palmer: *A Linguistic Study of the English Verb*, Longmans Green
& Co.; 1965.
5. The terms 'temperer, apex, limiter' are ultimately derived from
Mr. G. J. Turner, I believe. I was given the terms at a linguistic
conference; they seemed very apt, and so I have taken the liberty of
retaining them here.
6. Phased predicators: this section owes much to the books by F. R.
Palmer and J. M. Sinclair already mentioned, and to discussions
with various colleagues.
7. *It was John who . . .*, example from M. A. K. Halliday: 'Some
Notes on Deep Grammar', *Journal of Linguistics*, *Vol. 2, No. 1.*
8. O. Jespersen: *A Modern English Grammar on Historical Principles*,
Copenhagen; 1940.
9. The section on transitivity systems is perhaps of doubtful value
as presented here. It follows closely, and in effect is my reading of,

a series of articles by M. A. K. Halliday in the *Journal of Linguistics, Vol. 3, Nos 1 & 2*; and *Vol. 4, No. 2*. Halliday acknowledges that what is contained in these articles is inadequate, though not invalid. He is preparing an extended monograph on the subject (private communication). I agree with this (and other linguists are at present concerned with problems of transitivity from differing viewpoints), but it does seem to me that the 'actor–action–goal' view of transitivity is valid as far as it goes, and brings out further problems and directions for the grammar. The quotation is taken from the first of these articles.

10. See J. Anderson: 'Ergative and Nominative in English', *Journal of Linguistics, Vol. 4, No. 1*.

11. This consideration of gender derives ultimately from J. C. Catford; see B. Strang: *The Structure of English*, Arnold; 1962 (p. 95 and note of acknowledgement there).

12. The presentation of tense given here is based on lectures by M. A. K. Halliday. Professor Halliday is at present preparing a paper 'On Finiteness, Tense, and Modality in the English Verb' which will provide a full description of this system of tense. (Private communication.)

Bibliography

FIRTH, J. R. 'A Synopsis of Linguistic Theory', in *Studies in Linguistic Analysis*, (Ed.) J. R. Firth, Oxford: Basil Blackwell (special volume of the Philological Society), 1957

—— *Papers in Linguistics 1934–1951*, London: Oxford U.P., 1957

—— *Selected Papers of J. R. Firth*, (Ed.) F. R. Palmer, London: Longman's Linguistics Library, 1968

HALLIDAY, M. A. K. 'Some Aspects of Systematic Description and Comparison in Grammatical Analysis', in *Studies in Linguistic Analysis*, Oxford: Basil Blackwell, 1957

—— 'Categories of the Theory of Grammar', in *Word*, Vol. 17, No. 3, 1961

—— 'Class in Relation to the Axes of Chain and Choice in Language', in *Linguistics 2*, 1963

—— 'Some Notes on Deep Grammar', in *Journal of Linguistics*, Vol. 2, No. 1, 1966

—— 'Notes on Transitivity and Theme I–III', in *Journal of Linguistics*, Vol. 3, No. 1, Vol. 3, No. 2, Vol. 4, No. 2, 1967/8

—— 'Language Structure and Language Function', in *New Horizons in Linguistics*, (Ed.) J. Lyons, London: Penguin Books, 1970

—— 'Functional Diversity in Language, as seen from a consideration of Modality and Mood in English', in *Foundations of Language*, 6, 1970

HUDDLESTON, R. D. 'Rank and Depth', in *Language*, 41, 1965

HUDSON, R. A. 'Constituency in a Systemic Description of the English Clause', in *Lingua*, Vol. 18, No. 3, 1967

DAVIES, E. 'Some Notes on English Clause Types', in *Transactions of the Philological Society*, 1967

MCINTOSH, A. and HALLIDAY, M. A. K. *Patterns of Language: Papers in General, Descriptive and Applied Linguistics*, London: Longman's Linguistics Library, 1966

MCINTOSH, A., HALLIDAY, M. A. K. and STREVENS, P. *The Linguistic Sciences and Language Teaching*, London: Longman's Linguistics Library, 1964

PALMER, F. R. *A Linguistic Study of the English Verb*, London: Longman's Linguistics Library, 1966

MITCHELL, T. E. 'Syntagmatic Relations in Linguistic Analysis', in *Transactions of the Philological Society*, 1958

Other references:

QUIRK, R. *The Use of English*, London: Longmans, Green & Co., 1st edition 1962, 2nd edition 1968

BLOOMFIELD, L. *Language*, London: Allen & Unwin Ltd., 1935

ANDERSON, J. 'Ergative and Nominative in English', in *Journal of Linguistics*, Vol. 4, No. 1, 1968

GREENBERG, J. H. *Essays in Linguistics*, University of Chicago Press, 1957

JESPERSEN, O. *A Modern English Grammar on Historical Principles*, Copenhagen, 1940

Index